Word Study in Action

Words Their Way

Teacher Resource Guide Ⓑ

Donald R. Bear • Marcia Invernizzi • Francine Johnston

CELEBRATION PRESS

Pearson Learning Group

Program Reviewers

Pam Brown, Teacher
Sayre School
Lexington, KY

Katrina Currier, Language Arts Curriculum Coordinator
San Francisco Day School
San Francisco, CA

Kathy Lamkin, Teacher
Tuscan Elementary School
Maplewood, NJ

Shellie Winter, Teacher
Ponce de Leon Elementary School
Clearwater, FL

The following people have contributed to the development of this product:
Art and Design: Tricia Battipede, Sherri Hieber-Day, Dorothea Fox, Denise Ingrassia, David Mager, Judy Mahoney, Elbaliz Mendez
Editorial: Leslie Feierstone-Barna, Linda Dorf, Linette Mathewson, Tracey Randinelli
Inventory: Yvette Higgins
Marketing: Christine Fleming
Production/Manufacturing: Alan Dalgleish
Publishing Operations: Jennifer Van Der Heide

ISBN 0-7652-6749-7
Printed in the United States of America
    3 4 5 6 7 8 9 10   08 07 06 05

Celebration Press
Pearson Learning Group

1-800-321-3106
www.pearsonlearning.com

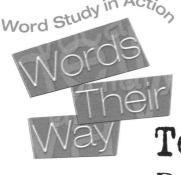

Word Study in Action

Words Their Way

Teacher Resource Guide (B)

Donald R. Bear • Marcia Invernizzi • Francine Johnston

Contents

Program Overview

Teachers have been using *Words Their Way: Word Study for Phonics, Vocabulary, and Spelling Instruction* (Merrill/Prentice Hall, 1996, 2000, 2004), authored by noted researchers Donald R. Bear, Marcia Invernizzi, Francine Johnston, and Shane Templeton, to teach children phonics, spelling, and vocabulary for the past eight years. This powerful approach to word study teaches children to look closely at words to discover the regularities and conventions of English orthography needed to read and spell. The success of this instruction has led Pearson Learning Group to publish *Words Their Way: Word Study in Action*, the official companion, in a ready-to-use format. This multi-component curriculum helps children increase their knowledge of the spelling patterns and the meanings of specific words and generalize this knowledge to the English spelling system.

How Does Words Their Way: Word Study in Action Work?

The heart of the *Words Their Way: Word Study in Action* program is the **sort**, or the process of grouping sounds, words, and pictures that represent words into specific categories. Word sorting includes teacher-directed instruction as well as independent learning. You begin by demonstrating how to sort picture or word cards by sound or pattern. Later, as children sort word cards or picture cards on their own, they make discoveries and generalizations about the conventions of English orthography. They compare and contrast word features and discover similarities and differences within the categories.

Words Their Way: Word Study in Action consists of 36 sorts in Levels K, B, and C, and 38 sorts in Level A. Each sort is designed to be completed in a week. The sequence of the program is based on the alphabet, pattern, and meaning principles that have been observed in children's spelling. *Words Their Way: Word Study in Action* provides the following important hands-on experiences:

- Comparing and contrasting words by sound so that children can categorize similar sounds and associate them consistently with letters and letter combinations. For example, words spelled with -*at* (*rat, sat, fat*) are compared with words spelled with -*ot* (*not, lot, rot*).
- Comparing and contrasting words by consistent spelling patterns associated with categories of sound. For example, words spelled with -*oi* (*join, soil, coin*) are compared with words spelled with -*oy* (*joy, annoy, coy*).
- Categorizing words by meaning, use, and parts of speech

Words Their Way: Word Study in Action and "Reading First"

In April 2000, the National Reading Panel (NRP) issued a report describing how children learn to read. As an offshoot of that report, and as part of No Child Left Behind (NCLB), the Reading First (RF) initiative was established. Reading First focuses on five areas of reading instruction needed to successfully teach children to read—phonemic awareness, phonics, fluency, comprehension, and vocabulary. *Words Their Way: Word Study in Action* addresses the following essential reading components:

Phonemic awareness: Children identify picture names that begin with the same sound, isolate and say the first sound in picture names, identify and categorize onsets and rhymes, and build words by substituting consonant sounds and blending them with various word families.

Phonics: Children sort words by beginning and ending consonants, consonant blends or digraphs, CVC short-vowel rhyming families, and long vowel patterns. They learn to analyze letter-sound relationships and how to use spelling patterns to decode words in reading and spell words in writing.

Fluency: Children listen as you model fluent reading of poems and books that contain the phonics elements they are learning and that leads to fluency in letter and word recognition.

Words Their Way: Word Study in Action also supports the following:

Vocabulary: Children learn the meanings of words by sorting them according to categories, such as living and nonliving things. Words are categorized by meaning and parts of speech.

Comprehension: Children apply skills they've learned through shared reading of texts from the *Words Their Way* Library, and become empowered to read with greater understanding.

About the Authors

Donald R. Bear is director of the E. L. Cord Center for Learning and Literacy in the College of Education at the University of Nevada, Reno. He teaches in the literacy center and meets with schools and districts to plan literacy programs. He is a former preschool and elementary teacher whose recent research includes the study of literacy development in different languages.

Marcia Invernizzi is a professor of reading education at the Curry School of Education at the University of Virginia. She is also the director of the McGuffey Reading Center, where she teaches the clinical practica in diagnosis and remediation, doctoral seminars in reading research, and a course in word study. She is formerly an English and reading teacher and is the principal author of Phonological Awareness Literacy Screening (PALS).

Francine Johnston is an associate professor at the School of Education at the University of North Carolina at Greensboro, where she teaches courses in reading, language arts, and children's literature. She taught in public schools for sixteen years as a first grade teacher and reading specialist. Her research interests include the relationship between spelling and reading achievement.

Program Components

Words Their Way: Word Study in Action supports the routines established in *Words Their Way: Word Study for Phonics, Vocabulary, and Spelling Instruction* by providing the materials you need for each sort in a ready-to-use format. Picture and word cards, sorting grids, game boards, and reading materials that contain the same spelling patterns and vocabulary they sorted are all provided.

Words Their Way: Word Study in Action contains the following components:

Each level of the program (K, A, B, C) features a consumable **Word Study Notebook**. The Word Study Notebook contains a four-page lesson for each sort, including picture and/or word cards for children to cut out and a grid onto which children sort and paste the picture/word cards. Each lesson also contains a written activity that gives children practice in the skill that corresponds to the lesson's sort. The letter to families on the inside front cover of the Word Study Notebook connects classroom word-study work with practice at home, promoting family involvement. An **envelope** is provided for children to store their picture/word cards for the week. A convenient self-stick strip allows the envelope to be attached to the inside back cover of the Word Study Notebook.

The **Big Book of Rhymes**, included with Levels K, A, and B of *Words Their Way: Word Study in Action*, contains a poem for each lesson. Words in the poems reflect the skill covered in the corresponding sort. High-interest, engaging illustrations accompany each poem and can be used to foster discussion.

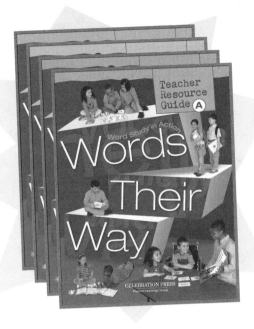

All four levels of *Words Their Way: Word Study in Action* feature a **Teacher Resource Guide**, containing lesson plans for each sort in the level, along with an explanation of how to use the program and tips for progress monitoring and classroom management.

The **Teacher Resource CD** is an interactive resource provided with all four levels of *Words Their Way: Word Study in Action.* The CD-ROM contains a variety of materials that can be printed and integrated into classroom word-study instruction:

- **Picture/word cards** can be used to demonstrate each sort in a level.

- **Games and activities** give children additional practice in each week's sort skill.

- **Build, Blend, and Extend activities** in Levels K and A focus on building new words and blending word parts for additional phonics, phonemic awareness, and word-study practice.

- **Sorts** from the last half of the previous level and the first half of the next level help you address the needs of children who may require extra practice or who may be ready for more challenging material.

- **Blank templates** allow you and your students to create your own sorts and games.

Most sorts in Levels K, A, B, and C are aligned to corresponding little books from the ***Words Their Way* Library.** Each book features a skill covered in the week's sort. Stories are age-appropriate and appealing.

An optional **storage box** with labeled file folders lets you organize all of the materials for each sort, as well as your copy of the Word Study Notebook and the Teacher Resource Guide.

Developmental Stages

The methodology of *Words Their Way: Word Study for Phonics, Vocabulary, and Spelling Instruction* reflects a progression of stages that describe children's spelling behavior as they move from one level of word knowledge to the next. The stages cited in the book make it easier to understand and recognize the basic strategies that children use to spell. In *Words Their Way: Word Study in Action*, these stages have been adapted to correspond to specific levels within the program. Levels K, A, B, and C of *Words Their Way: Word Study in Action* cover four spelling stages: Emergent, Letter Name-Alphabetic, Within Word Pattern, and Syllables and Affixes.

Emergent Spelling (Level K/On-level Kindergarten) During this stage, children learn to recognize and write the letters of the alphabet. They play with the sounds in words and letters. Most of the sound play focuses on beginning and rhyming sounds. Through most of Level K, children sort pictures by rhyme and beginning sounds. By the end of the level, children acquire an understanding of the concept of words and begin to match picture cards to the words that represent their names.

Letter Name-Alphabetic Spelling (Level A/On-level Grade 1) At the beginning of this stage, children apply the alphabet principles primarily to consonants. By the end of the stage, children are able to represent most short vowel patterns, consonant digraphs, and consonant blends correctly. In Level A, children sort pictures and/or words by beginning consonants, digraphs, and blends, and by word families.

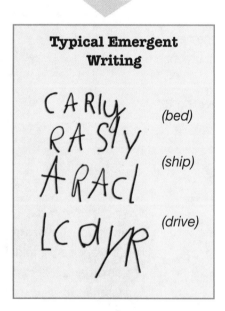

Typical Emergent Writing

CARly (bed)

RASly (ship)

ARACl

LCdyR (drive)

Typical Letter Name-Alphabetic Spelling

BAD for *bed*
SEP or SHP for *ship*
FOT for *float*
LOP for *lump*

Examples	Emergent (Level K)
bed	
ship	
float	
train	
cattle	
cellar	

Within Word Pattern Spelling (Level B/On-level Grade 2) Children at the beginning of this stage spell most single-syllable, short vowel words correctly. Then children move away from the sound-by-sound approach of the letter name and begin to include patterns or chunks of letter sequences that relate to sound and meaning. In Level B, children begin to sort words by long vowel patterns.

Syllables and Affixes Spelling (Level C/On-level Grade 3) By this stage, children already spell most one-syllable short and long vowel words correctly. The focus of instruction shifts to multisyllabic words and patterns. In *Words Their Way: Word Study in Action*, children sort Level C words by specific vowel combinations, inflected endings (including plurals, *-ing*, and *-ed*), and vowel patterns in accented syllables.

Typical Within Word Pattern Spelling
TRANE for train
SOPE for soap
DRIEV for drive
SPOLE for spoil

Typical Syllables and Affixes Spelling
SELLER for *cellar*
DAMIGE for *damage*
RIDDING for *riding*
FUNY for *funny*

Stages of Spelling in *Words Their Way*

Letter Name-Alphabetic (Level A)					Within Word Pattern (Level B)				Syllables and Affixes (Level C)			
b bd	bad				bed							
s sp	sep	shep			ship							
f ft	fot	flot	flott		flowt	floaut	flote	float				
t trn	jran	tan	chran	tran	teran	traen	trane	train				
c kd	catl		cadol			catel	catol		cattel	cattle		
s slr	salr		celr		saler	celer			seler	celler	seler	cellar

Scope and Sequence

The following chart shows the skills presented in *Words Their Way: Word Study in Action*. The first column lists the skills. The subsequent columns indicate the *Words Their Way* level or levels at which the skills are covered.

Skill	Level K	Level A	Level B	Level C
Concept Sorts	•			
Rhyming Sorts	•			
Concepts of Word in Print	•			
Letter Recognition	•			
Beginning Sounds	•			
Ending Sounds **t, x**	•			
Short Vowels **a, e, i, o, u**	•	•	•	
Short Vowel Word Families	•	•		
Beginning Consonants		•		
Consonant Digraphs		•	•	
Consonant Blends		•	•	
Beginning Sounds **k, wh, qu, tw**		•		
Short Vowel Words With Beginning Consonant Digraphs		•		
Short Vowel Words With Beginning Blends		•		
Short Vowel Words With Final Blends		•		
Long Vowels **a, e, i, o, u**		•	•	
Final /k/ Sound Spelled **-ck, -ke,** or **-k**			•	
Consonant Digraphs With Short Vowels			•	
Consonant Digraphs With Long Vowels			•	
Consonant Digraphs Plus **r**-Blends and **squ**			•	
CVVC Patterns **ai, oa, ee, ea**			•	•

Skill	Level K	Level A	Level B	Level C
Diphthongs			•	•
Ambiguous Vowel Sounds			•	•
Long Vowel Patterns			•	•
r-Influenced Vowel Patterns			•	•
Silent Beginning Consonants **kn, wr, gn**			•	
Triple **r**-blends **scr, str, spr**			•	•
Vowel Digraphs			•	
Hard and Soft **c** and **g**			•	•
Word Endings **-ce, -ve, -se**			•	•
Word Endings **-dge, -ge**				•
Word Endings **-tch, -ch**				•
Homophones				•
Contractions				•
Plural Endings				•
Inflected Endings **-ing**				•
Inflected Endings **-ed**				•
Unusual Past Tense Words				•
Compound Words				•
Syllable Juncture				•
Open and Closed Syllables and Inflected Endings				•
Long Vowel Patterns in Accented Syllables				•

Research Base

With purposeful reading, writing, listening, and speaking, words are learned. Even more words are acquired when they are explicitly examined to discover relationships among sounds, spelling patterns, and meanings.

Words Their Way: Word Study in Action increases knowledge of the spelling patterns and the meaning of specific words. Children learn to compare, contrast, and classify categories of sounds and words.

Research	Findings	Put Into Action With *Words Their Way*
Read, 1971, 1975	• Students' spellings reveal systematic, phonetic logic underlying preschoolers' categorization of English speech sounds.	• Sorts focus on discovering similarities and differences in sounds, letters, letter-sounds, words, and meaning
Henderson, Estes, & Stonecash, 1972; Beers & Henderson, 1977; Henderson, 1981	• The spelling of primary school children reveals similar use of letter-name, alphabetic logic up to the next period of transition.	• Learning builds on what children know and what they are trying to negotiate. The Alphebetic principle is crucial to sorts for beginning readers.
Schlagal, 1992; Henderson & Templeton, 1986; Henderson, 1990; Invernizzi, Abouzeid & Gill, 1994	• Developmental study of spelling in grades one through six reveals three discernable phases of orthographic understandings: alphabet, pattern, and meaning.	• Word study progresses through systematic instruction in sound, alphabetic letter-sound correspondences, spelling patterns, and spelling-meaning connections.
Morris & Perney, 1984; Bear & Barone, 1989; Ganske, 1999	• Developmental spelling analyses in the fall of the school year are reliable and valid predictors of literacy proficiency at the end of the school year.	• *Words Their Way* assessments place students in appropriate position in scope and sequence of *Words Their Way: Word Study in Action.*
Weber & Henderson, 1989; Hayes, 2004	• Fourth grade students assigned to word sort group significantly outperform control group on standardized measures of reading and spelling.	• Students learn to recognize, decode, and write spelling patterns.
Ehri, 1997; Ellis, 1997; Perfetti, 1997; Perfetti, 2003	• There is an interaction and integration of reading and spelling development. Students' orthographic knowledge develops in predictable phases.	• *Words Their Way: Word Study in Action* includes word study activities that are beneficial to both reading and spelling development at the best instructional level.

*See page 23 for all research references.

Research	Findings	Put Into Action With *Words Their Way*
Zutell & Rasinski, 1989; Johnston, 1998; Bear, 1992; Invernizzi, 1992; Templeton & Bear, 1992	• Orthographic knowledge significantly predicts sight word acquisition, word recognition, and oral reading fluency. Relationships among spelling, reading, and writing are reciprocal and symbiotic.	• Students categorize words by sound, pattern, and meaning, then search for other words that work the same way in poems from the Big Book of Rhymes and books from the *Words Their Way* Library. Word recognition is enhanced when words are studied in isolation.
August & Hakuta, 1997; Bear & Helman, 2004; Bear, Templeton, Helman, & Baren, 2003; Fashola, Drum, Mayer, & Kang, 1996; Helman & Baren, 2003; Helman, L. A., 2004; Weber & Longhi-Chirlin, 2001; Zutell & Allen, 1988; Shen & Bear, 2000	• Students' first oral and written languages influence the way they learn to read and spell in English. Spelling errors among English language learners are predictable.	• *Words Their Way: Word Study in Action* highlights the specific needs of students at different points in their literacy development. Ways to tailor sorts to the language and developmental needs of students are provided for each sort and lesson.
Worthy & Invernizzi, 1989; Templeton & Bear, 2000, Sawyer, Lipa-Wade, Kim, Ritenour, & Knight, 1997; Cantrell, 2000	• Children who have learning disabilities, speak nonstandard dialects, or experience language delays demonstrate the same types of spelling confusions, and they benefit from word study at their instuctional levels.	• Alternate sorting activities and vocabulary building, alerts and instructions for English language learners, and teacher tips are provided with each week's work so the skills can be clarified, practiced, and extended.
Morris, Blanton, Blanton, Nowacek, & Perney, 1995; Hayes, 2004	• Teaching low achieving spellers at their "instructional levels" yields greater gains than control group students who received grade-level instruction regardless of their instructional level.	• Ongoing spell checks allow for flexible grouping and differentiated phonics, spelling, and vocabulary instruction.
Templeton & Morris, 2001; Invernizzi & Hayes, 2004	• Effective word study instruction reveals the historical structures inherent in English orthography.	• Sorts and lessons focus on the systematic progression of alphabet, pattern, and meaning.

Using Words Their Way In Your Literacy Block

Words Their Way: Word Study in Action can be used in conjunction with other reading, spelling, and vocabulary programs in your classroom. Introductory lessons may take about 20 minutes, but subsequent activities will last only about 10 to 15 minutes a day and do not require much teacher direction. Word study can fit easily into many parts of the day.

Options for Using Words Their Way

Words Their Way: Word Study in Action can be used in a variety of classroom environments.

- **Guided reading:** If you use a guided reading program, *Words Their Way: Word Study in Action* is an excellent way to incorporate phonics into the curriculum.

- **Basal reading:** If you use a basal reading program, *Words Their Way: Word Study in Action* is an effective supplemental phonics resource that can be matched to the phonics skills you are teaching.

- **Stand-alone:** *Words Their Way: Word Study in Action* can also be used as a stand-alone spelling and phonics program.

Getting Started

One of the benefits of the *Words Their Way: Word Study in Action* program is that all of the components you need for a week's worth of instruction are easily accessible. As you begin each week, mark the pages that correspond to the week's sort in your copy of the Word Study Notebook and in the Big Book of Rhymes. Set aside copies of the little book title from the *Words Their Way* Library you'll be using during the week, and print out the picture/word cards; game; Build, Blend, and Extend activity (if applicable); and any other materials you'll need. You may find it helpful to use file folders labeled with the different sort numbers to organize your instructional materials. A file folder is also ideal to use as a base for a game board; simply attach the two game board halves to an open file folder.

Decide where children will work. Space is needed for group work, individual work, and partner work. Separate areas on the floor or at tables in one part of the classroom to work with groups as they sort and discuss their results. Encourage other children to continue to work at their desk or in other areas of the room.

For more ideas about organizing word study in your classroom, see *Words Their Way: Word Study for Phonics, Vocabulary, and Spelling Instruction*, Chapter Three.

How to Group Children

Words Their Way: Word Study in Action is designed to be used with small groups of five to ten children. Many teachers incorporate word study groups into small-group reading levels. Administering the Spell Check (found at the end of the Word Study Notebook) that corresponds to a specific skill strand can help you structure groups according to proficiency. Another easy way to group students is to determine whether they fall into the early, middle, or late stage of a particular level. The following chart highlights what you may see children use but confuse in their writing at different points in each *Words Their Way: Word Study in Action* level. Use the chart to help you decide where to place each child.

	Early	Middle	Late
Level K (On-level Grade K)	• Drawing and scribbling for writing	• Letters, numbers, and letter-like forms • Writing may wrap from right to left at the end of a line	• Substitutions of letters that sound, feel, and look alike: *Bp, Db*
Level A (On-level Grade 1)	• Letters based on point of articulation: J, JRF for *drive* • Often long vowels by letter name	• Substitutions of letter name closest in point of articulation for short vowels • Some consonant blends and digraphs	• Substitutions of common patterns for low frequency short vowels: COT for *caught*
Level B (On-level Grade 2)	• Long vowel markers: SNAIK for *snake*, FELE for *feel*	• Long vowel markers: NITE for *night* • Consonant patterns: SMOCK for *smoke* • Inventive substitutions in frequent, unstressed syllable patterns: TEACHAUR for *teacher* • *-ed* and other common inflections: MARCHT for *marched*, BATID for *batted*	• Low frequency long vowel words: HIEGHT for *height* • *-ed* and other common inflections • Common Latin suffixes are spelled phonetically: ATTENSHUN for *attention*
Level C (On-level Grade 3)	• Consonant doubling: HOPING for *hopping* • Long vowel patterns in accented syllable: PERAIDING or PERADDING for *parading* • Reduced vowel in unaccented syllable: CIRCUL for *circle* • Doubling and *e* drop: AMAZZING for *amazing*	• Some silent letters: EMFASIZE for *emphasize*, INDITEMENT for *indictment*	• Some suffixes and prefixes: ATTENSION for *attention*, PERTEND for *pretend* • Vowel alternation in derivationally related pairs: COMPUSITION for *composition* • Consonant alternations in derivationally related pairs: SPACIAL for *spatial*

Walk Through the Week

The lesson plan for each sort is presented in a logical and easy-to-follow way. It provides additional ideas for sorting, building vocabulary, helping English language learners, and using challenge words.

The **pictures and words** in the lesson are clearly identified.

Many lessons include additional **Challenge Words** that coordinate with the skills in the lesson for additional practice that is a bit more challenging.

Objectives identify the skill covered and describe what children accomplish in the lesson.

A list of **Materials** lets you see at a glance where to find each component used in the lesson.

Sort 8 — Word Families -op, -ot, -og

Objectives

- To identify short o rhyming words
- To identify and sort pictures and words with -op, -ot, or -og

Materials

 Big Book of Rhymes, Level A, "One Hot Day," page 15

 Teacher Resource CD, Level A

 Word Study Notebook, Level A, pages 31–34

Words Their Way Library, Level A, *Lost in the Fog*

 Teacher Resource CD, Level A, Rock Hop Game

Pictures/Words

-op	-ot	-og
mop	pot	frog
hop	dot	hog
top	hot	log
pop	cot	jog

Challenge Words

chop	slot	bog
plop	spot	cog
flop	plot	clog
shop	trot	

Day 1 — Introduce the Sort

In Levels K, A, and B, children listen as you read aloud a poem from the Big Book of Rhymes. They identify and discuss words in the poem that correspond to the lesson's skill. In the second half of the day's word-study session, you use the picture/word cards located on the Teacher Resource CD to model how to perform the week's sort.

Day 1 — Introduce the Sort

Whole Group

Read a Rhyme: "One Hot Day"

Introduce short o rhyming words by reading the poem "One Hot Day." As you read, emphasize the words that rhyme *(spot, hot; do, too)*. As children find the rhyming words in the poem, write them in a column on the chalkboard or on chart paper. Help children understand that these words rhyme because they end with the same sound and letters. Read the poem again, omitting the last word of each line, and have children supply the missing word.

Introduce Picture/Word Sort -op, -ot, -og

Print and cut apart the picture/word cards for Sort 8 from the Teacher Resource CD. Introduce the pictures and words, defining in context any words that are unfamiliar, such as *top, cot, hog, and jog*. Then demonstrate for children how to sort the pictures into -op, -ot, and -og word families. Ask children to describe how the pictures in each column are alike. *(They rhyme.)* Then introduce the word cards, and ask children to match each word card to its picture.

30

Day 2 — Practice the Sort

Whole Group/Independent

 You may want to begin Days 2–5 by rereading the rhyme from Day 1. Then review the previous day's sort demonstration. Help children tear out page 31 from their Word Study Notebook and cut apart the cards.

Have children work independently or with a partner to sort the picture cards by ending sound, and then match the words and pictures in each word family. Have children say the names of the pictures and read the words as they work.

Alternative Sort: Identify My Category

When children are comfortable with this week's sort, re-sort the pictures or words into groups of living and nonliving things. Begin by sorting two or three of the pictures into the categories. When you pick up the next picture or word card, invite children to identify where it will go. Continue to do this until all the cards have been sorted and children are able to identify the categories.

Day 2 — Practice the Sort

Review the sort with children and direct them to cut apart the picture/word cards in their Word Study Notebook. Children then sort their cards according to specific categories that reflect the sort skill.

An **Alternative Sort** provides another way for children to sort their picture/word cards.

Find Words in Context

A corresponding book from the *Words Their Way* Library provides opportunities for both shared and independent reading, as children identify words from the text that reflect the target skill.

Apply the Skill

Children demonstrate what they have learned by completing a writing activity found in the Word Study Notebook.

Find Words in Context

Whole Group/Independent/Partner

Have children re-sort their cards. Then read *Lost in the Fog* with children. Have children listen for and identify any words that end with *-op, -ot,* or *-og*.

Have children look through their word cards to find words that match words in the text. Then have them read the story independently and find other words in the story that end with *-op, -ot,* or *-og*.

Apply the Skill

Independent/Partner

Have children sort their cards again. Then have children turn to page 34 in their Word Study Notebook. Read aloud the directions, and encourage children work independently or with a partner to write words that end with *-og, -ot,* or *-op*.

Complete the Sort

Whole Group/Independent

Paste in Place

Encourage children to sort and match their pictures and words into *-op, -ot,* and *-og* word families. Then have them turn to page 33 in their Word Study Notebook and paste the pictures and matching words in the correct column for each word family.

Play the Game

When children are finished, they may play the Rock Hop game. (See the Teacher Resource CD for the game board, playing cards, and directions.)

Building Vocabulary

If children are unfamiliar with the word *jog*, explain that it means "to run at a slow, steady pace." Invite children to stand up and practice jogging in place.

ESL/ELL English Language Learners

Review the pictures and words with children. You may need to explain that a *hog* is similar to a *pig*, that a *cot* is a small bed, and that *jog* is the same as *run*. Have children pronounce each word to be sure they are differentiating among the three endings *-op, -ot,* and *-og*.

Challenge Words Activity

Ask children to find other words that end with *-op, -ot,* or *-og*. (If children need prompting, make suggestions from the Challenge Words list on the facing page.) Then have children make word cards for these new words. They can work in small groups to sort the words into categories.

Teacher Tip

During a second or repeated sort, do not correct children when they place a picture or word in the wrong column. Wait until they have completed the sort, and have them read the words in each column to check them. If they still don't find the misplaced picture or word, tell them which column it is in, and have them find it.

You may wish to use the Sort 8 **Build, Blend, and Extend**. (See the Teacher Resource CD.)

31

Building Vocabulary

provides meanings for unfamiliar words and pictures and suggests a strategy to help children understand words they don't know.

English Language Learners

presents extra support for children through additional exploration of vocabulary in context, unfamiliar blends and vowel sounds, and other concepts that English language learners may find difficult.

Challenge Words Activity

provides a sorting activity that can be used with the Challenge Words listed on the previous page.

Teacher Tip

gives a suggestion designed to aid in areas such as instruction, assessment, and classroom management.

Complete the Sort

Children sort their cards one final time and paste them into place on the grid in the Word Study Notebook. In the second half of the day's word study session, children play a game found on the Teacher Resource CD, such as Bingo! or Go Fish, that helps them apply the skills in the sort.

Meeting Individual Differences

Recognizing not only a child's spelling stage, but also his or her level within the stage, will help you know when to teach what. Children in Grade 1, for example, may be in the early, middle, or late level of the Letter Name-Alphabetic stage, or they may be in the late level of the previous stage (Emergent) or the early level of the next stage (Within Word Pattern).

To address this issue, sorts for the second half of the previous level and the first half of the next level are included (when applicable) on a specific level's Teacher Resource CD, ensuring that *Words Their Way: Word Study in Action* provides flexibility for all the varied instructional levels in your classroom.

In addition, you may find that your students can move through the sorts very quickly. In that case, you may wish to use more than one complete level kit in your classroom.

English language learners Each lesson plan in *Words Their Way: Word Study in Action* provides a suggestion for adapting the lesson to better fit the needs of English language learners. The tips cover a range of concepts that English language learners may find difficult, including letters and sounds that may be different from those in their native language, unusual spelling patterns, and vocabulary in context.

Family involvement The inside front cover of the Word Study Notebook provides an at-home activity for families to do with their children each night from Monday through Thursday.

Progress Monitoring and Using the Spell Checks

To monitor children's word-study progress, you can include a combination of writing samples, observations during oral reading, and analysis of spelling errors in formal assessments. The Spell Checks provided in each level of *Words Their Way: Word Study in Action* are another valuable assessment tool. Spell Checks are provided in the back of the Word Study Notebook. As children complete each series of skills, administer the corresponding Spell Check to determine what they have learned and what they do not understand. Then use the results of the Spell Check to plan for individual or small-group instruction.

Spell Check 1: Long and Short Vowel Sounds should be used after completing Sort 9. This Spell Check assesses children's ability to identify short and long vowel sounds. Watch for these types of errors: If children have trouble discriminating between short *a* and short *e*, review Sort 3 and Sort 7 with children; if children have trouble discriminating between long *o* and long *u*, have them review Sorts 5 and 6. These are the 20 words assessed:

1. bag, 2. toe, 3. fox, 4. leaf, 5. train, 6. tube, 7. frog, 8. smell, 9. crab, 10. nest, 11. dream, 12. duck, 13. cube, 14. crib, 15. map, 16. fruit, 17. smile, 18. dive, 19. clock, 20. crane

Spell Check 2: CVVC Long Vowel Patterns should be used after completing Sort 15. This Spell Check assesses children's ability to write one-syllable long-vowel words. Watch for these types of errors: if children write *ran* for *rain,* review Sort 10; if children write *brom* for *broom,* review Sort 11. These are the 15 words assessed:

1. leaf, 2. suit, 3. beach, 4. rain, 5. road, 6. teeth, 7. snake, 8. feet, 9. queen, 10. soap 11. fruit, 12. broom, 13. tail, 14. coat, 15. spoon

Spell Check 3: Less Common Long Vowel Patterns should be used after completing Sort 21 with children. This Spell Check assesses children's ability to identify long vowel patterns and write one-syllable long-vowel words. Watch for these types of errors: if you see a pattern of writing CVCC words for CVVC words, review Sort 16, Sort 17, and Sort 20 with children; if children write CVCe words for CV or CVV Open Syllable words, have them review Sorts 19–20. Read aloud the following list of words:

1. fold, 2. wish, 3. try, 4. kind, 5. note, 6. stay, 7. child, 8. brain, 9. grow, 10. fight, 11. steep, 12. drew, 13. scene, 14. boat, 15. true, 16. blame, 17. school, 18. white, 19. close, 20. clue

Spell Check 4: r-Influenced Vowel Patterns should be used after completing Sort 27 with children. This Spell Check assesses children's ability to spell words with *r*-influenced vowel patterns. Watch for these types of errors: if children choose *chayre* for *chair,* review Sort 22 with children; if children choose *fourk* for *fork,* have them review Sort 25.

Name each picture, then read the sentence that goes with each picture (see next page). You may need the sentences to be sure students know which meaning the pictures are targeting, especially for the homophones. Tell your students to circle the word under each picture that matches the meaning of the sentence and that contains the correct spelling pattern.

1. **First.** When you win the race, you get **first** prize **First.**

2. **Corn. Corn** is a type of grain or cereal plant that bears seed or kernels on large ears. **Corn.**

3. **Shirt.** A **shirt** is a piece of clothing for the upper part of the body. **Shirt.**

4. **Jar.** A **jar** is a glass or ceramic container with a wide mouth, usually without handles and used to store things like honey. **Jar.**

5. **Tire.** A **tire** is a covering for a wheel, usually made out of rubber. **Tire.**

6. **Fair.** A **fair** with lots of games and rides is coming to our town. **Fair.**

7. **Deer.** A male **deer** grows antlers and is sometimes called a buck. **Deer.**

8. **Worm.** A **worm** is an invertebrate animal that often has no arms or legs. **Worm.**

9. **Four.** The number **four** comes after the number three. **Four.**

10. **Chair.** A **chair** is a piece of furniture that makes it possible for people to sit. **Chair.**

11. **Stair.** You have to step up one **stair** to reach the door. **Stair.**

12. **Horse.** A **horse** is a large hoofed animal with a shorthaired coat, a long mane, and a long tail; often used for riding and carrying heavy loads. **Horse.**

13. **Three.** The number **three** comes after the number two. **Three.**

14. **Purse.** A **purse** is a bag that people use to carry things. **Purse.**

15. **Fork.** A **fork** is a three- or four-pronged utensil used for serving or eating food. **Fork.**

Spell Check 5: Diphthongs and Vowel Digraphs should be used after completing Sort 31 with children. This Spell Check assesses children's ability to identify vowel patterns and write words with *aw, au, ow, ou, oy,* and *oi.* Watch for these types of errors: if you see a pattern of writing *oi* for *oy,* (for example, *joyn* for *join*), review Sorts 29 and 31 with children; if children write *aw* for *au* (for example, *tawght* for *taught*), review Sort 30.

Say each word once in the following order, use it in a sentence, and then say the word again:

1. haul, 2. crawl, 3. drown, 4. couch, 5. fault, 6. joy, 7. growl, 8. toy, 9. mouth, 10. hawk, 11. moist, 12. taught, 13. Roy, 14. gown, 15. straw, 16. coin, 17. cloud, 18. ploy, 19. yawn, 20. spoil, 21. howl, 22. found, 23. launch, 24. broil

Spell Check 6A: Beginning Complex Consonant Clusters and **Spell Check 6B: Hard and Soft c and g and Word Endings -ce, -se, -ve** should be used after completing Sort 36 with children. This Spell Check assesses children's ability to spell and write words that begin or end with specific sounds. Watch for these types of errors: if children write *skream* for *scream* review Sort 33; if children write *-se* for *-ce* (for example, *pease* for *peace*), review Sort 36.

For Spell Check 6A, call out the words in the following order. Say the word, use it in a sentence to make sure your students understand what word you mean, and then say it again.

1. through, 2. shrub, 3. scream, 4. sprout, 5. squeeze, 6. straight, 7. throne, 8. scrape, 9. squirm, 10. string, 11. shrimp, 12. spread, 13. thrill, 14. scratch, 15. squash, 16. shrunk, 17. stress, 18. spruce, 19. shrink, 20. threw, 21. scrap, 22. stripe, 23. squint, 24. spray

For Spell Check 6B, call out the words in the following order. Say the word, use it in a sentence to make sure your students understand what word you mean, and then say it again.

1. peace, 2. calf, 3. twelve, 4. loose, 5. guess, 6. circle, 7. dance, 8. cart, 9. leave, 10. tease, 11. gym, 12. prince, 13. prove, 14. game, 15. wise, 16. since, 17. gem, 18. cent, 19. love, 20. those

Research Base References

August, D., & Hakuta, K. (Eds.). (1997). *Improving schooling for language minority students: A research agenda* (Committee on Developing a Research Agenda on the Education of Limited English Proficient and Bilingual Students–Board on Children, Youth and Families). Washington, D.C.: National Academy Press.

Bear, D. R. (1992). The prosody of oral reading and stage of word knowledge. In S. Templeton & D. Bear (Eds.), *Development of orthographic knowledge and the foundations of literacy: A memorial Festschrift for Edmund H. Henderson* (pp. 137–186). Hillsdale, NJ: Lawrence Erlbaum.

Bear, D. R. & Barone, D. (1989). Using children's spellings to group for word study and directed reading in the primary classroom. *Reading Psychology: An International Quarterly, 10*(3), 275–292.

Bear, D. R., & Helman, L. (2004). Word study for vocabulary development: An ecological perspective on instruction during the early stages of literacy learning. In J. F. Baumann & E. J. Kame'enui & (Eds.) *Vocabulary instruction: Research to practice* (pp. 139–158). NY: Guilford Press.

Bear, D. R., & Templeton, S., Helman, L., & Baren, T. (2003). Orthographic development and learning to read in different languages. In G. Garcia (Ed.), *English learners: Reaching the highest level of English literacy* (pp.71-95). Newark, DE: International Reading Association.

Bear, D. R., Truex, P., & Barone, D. (1989). In search of meaningful diagnoses: Spelling-by-stage assessment of literacy proficiency. *Adult Literacy and Basic Education, 13*(3), 165–185.

Beers, J., and Henderson, E. H. (1977, Fall) A study of developing orthographic concepts among first grade children. *Research in the Teaching of English, 11*(2),133–148.

Cantrell, R. J. (2001). Exploring the relationship between dialect and spelling for specific vocalic features in Appalachian first-grade children. *Linguistics and Education, 12*, 1–23.

Ehri, L. C. (1997). Learning to read and learning to spell are one and the same, almost. In C. A. Perfetti, L. Rieben, & M. Fayol (Eds.), *Learning to spell: Research, theory, and practice across languages* (pp. 237–269). Mahwah, NJ: Lawrence Erlbaum Associates.

Ellis, N. (1997). Interactions in the development of reading and spelling: Stages, strategies, and exchange of knowledge. In C. A. Perfetti & L. Rieben (Eds.), *Learning to spell: Research, theory, and practice across languages* (pp. 271–294). Mahwah, NJ: Lawrence Erlbaum Associates.

Fashola, O. S., Drum, P. A., Mayer, R. E., & Kang, S. (1996). A cognitive theory of orthographic transitioning: Predictable errors in how Spanish-speaking children spell English words. *American Educational Research Journal, 33*, 825–843.

Ganske, K. (1999). The developmental spelling analysis: A measure of orthographic knowledge. *Educational Assessment, 6*, 41–70.

Hayes, L. (2004). *A comparison of two systematic approaches to phonics and spelling instruction in beginning reading: A basal phonics program and word study.* Unpublished Doctoral Dissertation, University of Virginia, Charlottesville.

Helman, L. A. (2004). *Spanish-speaking students' development as beginning readers in English: Results from a statewide assessment of early literacy.* Unpublished doctoral dissertation, University of Nevada, Reno.

Henderson, E. H. (1981). *Learning to read and spell: The child's knowledge of words.* DeKalb: Northern Illinois Press.

Henderson, E. H. (1990). *Teaching spelling* (2nd ed.). Boston: Houghton Mifflin.

Henderson, E. H., Estes, T., & Stonecash, S. (1972). An exploratory study of word acquisition among first graders at midyear in a language experience approach. *Journal of Reading Behavior, 4*, 21–30.

Henderson, E. H., & Templeton, S. (1986) The development of spelling ability through alphabet, pattern, and meaning. *Elementary School Journal, 86*, 305–316.

Invernizzi, M. (1992). The vowel and what follows: A phonological frame of orthographic analysis. In S. Templeton & D. R. Bear (Eds.), *Development of orthographic knowledge and the foundations of literacy: A memorial Festschrift for Edmund H. Henderson* (pp. 106–136). Hillsdale, NJ: Lawrence Erlbaum.

Invernizzi, M., Abouzeid, M., & Gill, T. (1994). Using students' invented spellings as a guide for spelling instruction that emphasizes word study. *Elementary School Journal, 95*(2), 155–167.

Invernizzi, M. & Hayes, L. (2004) Developmental-spelling research: A systematic imperative. *Reading Research Quarterly, 39* (2), 216–228.

Johnston, F. R. (1998). The reader, the text, and the task: Learning words in first grade. *The Reading Teacher, 51*, 666–675.

Morris, D., Blanton, L., Blanton, W. E., Nowacek, J., & Perney, J. (1995). Teaching low-achieving spellers at their "instructional level." *Elementary School Journal, 96*, 163–178.

Morris, D., & Perney, J. (1984). Developmental spelling as a predictor of first-grade reading achievement. *Elementary School Journal, 84*, 441–457.

Perfetti, C. A. (1997). The psycholinguistics of spelling and reading. In C. A. Perfetti, L. Rieben, & M. Fayol (Eds.), *Learning to spell: Research, theory and practice across languages* (pp. 21–38). Mahwah, NJ: Lawrence Erlbaum Associates.

Perfetti, C. A. (2003). The universal grammar of reading. *Scientific Studies of Reading , 7*(1), 3–24.

Read, C. (1971). Pre-school children's knowledge of English phonology. *Harvard Educational Review, 41*(1), 1–34.

Read, C. (1975). *Children's categorization of speech sounds in English.* (NCTE Report No. 17) Urbana, IL: NCTE.

Sawyer, D. J., Lipa-Wade, S., Kim, J., Ritenour, D., & Knight, D. F. (1997). *Spelling errors as a window on dyslexia.* Paper presented at the 1997 annual convention of the American Educational Research Association, Chicago.

Schlagal, R. C. (1992). Patterns of orthographic development into the intermediate grades. In S. Templeton & D. R. Bear (Eds.), *Development of orthographic knowledge and the foundations of literacy: A memorial Festschrift for Edmund H. Henderson* (pp. 31–52). Hillsdale, NJ: Lawrence Erlbaum.

Shen, H., & Bear, D. R. (2000). The development of orthographic skills in Chinese children. *Reading and Writing: An Interdisciplinary Journal, 13*, 197–236.

Templeton, S., & Bear, D. R. (2000). What is the role of the speech-language pathologist in assessing and facilitating spelling skills? *Topics in Language Disorders, 20*, 88–93.

Templeton, S., & Bear, D. R. (Eds.). (1992). Teaching the lexicon to read and spell. In S. Templeton & D. R. Bear (Eds.), *Development of orthographic knowledge and the foundations of literacy: A memorial Festschrift for Edmund H. Henderson* (pp. 333–352). Hillsdale, NJ: Lawrence Erlbaum.

Templeton, S., & Morris, D. (2000). Spelling. In M. L. Kamil, P. B. Mosenthal, P. D. Pearson & R. Barr (Eds.), *Handbook of Reading Research: Volume III* (pp. 525–544). Mahwah, NJ: Lawrence Erlbaum Associates.

Weber, W., & Henderson, E. H. (1989). A computer-based program of word study: Effects on reading and spelling. *Reading Psychology, 10* (2), 157–162.

Weber, R. M. and Longhi-Chirlin, T. (2001). Beginning in English: The growth of linguistic and literate abilities in Spanish-speaking first graders. *Reading Research and Instruction. 4*, 1950.

Worthy, M. J., & Invernizzi, M. (1989). Spelling errors of normal and disabled students on achievement levels one through four: Instructional implications. *Bulletin of the Orton Society, 40*, 138–149.

Zutell, J. & Allen, J. (1988). The English spelling strategies of Spanish-speaking bilingual children. *TESOL Quarterly, 22*, 333–340.

Zutell, J. & Rasinski, T. (1989). Reading and spelling connections in third and fourth grade students. *Reading Psychology, 10*, 137–156.

Initial Consonant Blends br, sm, tr, sk, dr

Objectives:

- To identify the sounds of common initial consonant blends
- To identify and sort pictures whose names begin with *br, sm, tr, sk, dr*

Materials

Big Book of Rhymes, Level B, "Raindrop Song," page 5

Teacher Resource CD, Level B, Sort 1

Word Study Notebook, Level B, pages 3–6

Words Their Way Library, Level B, *The River Grows*

Teacher Resource CD, Level B, Spin and Blend

Pictures

sm	dr	tr	sk	br
smile	dress	tray	skunk	brush
smoke	drum	triangle	skis	bridge
smell	drawer	tree	skirt	broom
smock	drill	truck	skate	bride

Day 1 Introduce the Sort

Whole Group

Read a Rhyme: "Raindrop Song"

Read the poem "Raindrop Song" to children. As you read, emphasize words that begin with initial consonant blends *sm, dr, tr, sk,* or *br (small, drop, drizzle, trickles, track, sky, skip, bring)*. Divide the class into five groups, and assign a different initial consonant blend to each group. Slowly read the poem again. This time, instruct children to stand when they hear a word with the assigned blend.

Introduce Picture Sort *br, sm, tr, sk, dr*

Print out and cut apart the picture cards for Sort 1 from the Teacher Resource CD. Introduce and name the pictures. Define in context words that may be unfamiliar to children, such as *tray, drill,* and *smock*. Start to show children how to sort the pictures according to their initial consonant blend. Encourage children to help complete the sort. Then name the pictures in the first column and repeat the initial consonant blend common to each word. Continue with the remaining columns.

Day 2 Practice the Sort

Whole Group/Partner/Independent

You may want to begin Days 2–5 by reading the rhyme from Day 1. Then review the previous day's sort demonstration. Then help children remove page 3 from their Word Study Notebook and cut apart the cards.

Have children work independently or with a partner to name each picture and, using the grid on page 5 of their Word Study Notebook, sort the picture cards according to initial consonant blend.

Alternative Sort: Tool Shop

When children have completed this week's sort, briefly discuss tools. Explain that tools help us do jobs more easily. A tool can be as small as a pen or as big as a garden rake. Have children re-sort the cards according to whether or not they show pictures of tools.

Day 3

Find Words in Context

Whole Group

Have children re-sort their cards. Read *The River Grows* to children. Have children listen for words that begin with *br, sm, tr, sk,* or *dr.* Then ask children to answer some riddles about words in the story. Begin with a riddle about the word *trees.* "I'm thinking of a word that begins with the *tr* blend. The word names something that grows beside the river." Then ask a riddle about the word *drips.* "I'm thinking of a word that begins with the *dr* blend and tells how water sometimes moves." If you wish, have volunteers ask similar riddles about words in the story.

Day 4

Apply the Skill

Independent/Partner

Have children sort their cards again. As a class, brainstorm other words that begin with *br, sm, tr, sk,* or *dr.* Then have children turn to page 6 in their Word Study Notebook. Read aloud the directions, and have children work independently or with a partner to write words and draw pictures of things that begin with *br, sm, tr, sk,* or *dr.*

Day 5

Complete the Sort

Whole Group/Independent

Paste in Place

Have children turn to page 5 in their Word Study Notebook. Encourage children to say the name of each picture and then sort the picture cards according to the initial consonant blend *(br, sm, tr, sk, dr).* Then have them paste the pictures in the correct column for the initial consonant blend.

Play the Game

When children are finished, they may play Spin and Blend. (See the Teacher Resource CD for the game card, playing cards, spinner, and directions.)

Building Vocabulary

Explain that a *smock* is a loose shirt worn over one's usual clothes to protect them from getting dirty or stained. Some children may wear smocks to protect their clothes while doing art projects. If so, ask children to describe these smocks.

ESL/ELL ## English Language Learners

Review with children the picture cards, naming each picture. Give children examples of sentences with words that can be either verbs or nouns. "I found my skate. I skate on the ice." Then help children create their own sentences with words such as *smile, smell, dress,* and *brush.*

Teacher Tip

You may find that not all children sort the cards in the same way in this week's Alternative Sort (Tool Shop). For example, one child may place the picture of skis in the tool pile because skis help one move across the snow. Another child may think that skis are toys. Validate any position as long as the child can defend it.

Consonant Digraphs ch, sh, wh, th

Objectives:

- To identify the sounds of consonant digraphs
- To identify and sort pictures whose names begin or end with *ch, sh, wh,* or *th*

Materials

 Big Book of Rhymes, Level B, "Chuckie's Chore," page 7

 Teacher Resource CD, Level B, Sort 2

 Word Study Notebook, Level B, pages 7–10

 Words Their Way Library, Level B, *Rush, Rush, Rush*

 Teacher Resource CD, Level B, Digraph Dilemma

Pictures			
ch	*sh*	*wh*	*th*
beach	sheep	whistle	teeth
chick	dish	wheel	think
peach	shelf	wheat	thirty
cheese	fish	white	moth

Day 1 Introduce the Sort

Whole Group

 Read a Rhyme: "Chuckie's Chore"

Tell children that you will read a poem titled "Chuckie's Chore." Point out that the beginning sound of *Chuckie's* and *Chore* is spelled with two letters *(ch).* As you read the poem, have children listen for another *ch* word. *(chest)* Continue by having children identify words that begin or end with *sh, wh,* or *th. (stash, shelf, things, whisk)*

 Introduce Picture Sort *ch, sh, wh, th*

Print out and cut apart the picture cards for Sort 2 from the Teacher Resource CD. Introduce and name the pictures. Define in context picture names that may be unfamiliar to children, such as *chick, wheat,* and *moth.* Show children how to sort the pictures according to the digraphs *ch, sh, wh,* and *th.* Point out that sometimes the digraph is at the beginning of the word and sometimes it is at the end. Starting with the first column, name the pictures, one at a time, and have children repeat the words after you. Ask children to explain how all the words in the column are alike. Continue with the remaining columns.

Day 2 Practice the Sort

Whole Group/Partner/Independent

 You may want to begin Days 2–5 by reading the rhyme from Day 1. Then review the previous day's sort demonstration. Then help children tear out page 7 from their Word Study Notebook and cut apart the cards.

Have children work independently or with a partner to say the name of each picture and, using the grid on page 9 of their Word Study Notebook, sort the picture cards according to the consonant digraphs *ch, sh, wh,* and *th.*

> **Alternative Sort: Beginning or End**
> When children are comfortable with this week's sort, have them re-sort the cards into two piles. One pile should have pictures whose names begin with a consonant digraph. The other pile should have pictures whose names end with a consonant digraph.

Day 3

Find Words in Context

Whole Group

Have children re-sort their cards. Read *Rush, Rush, Rush* to the class. Then leaf through the book, one page at a time, as children identify the things the people in the story are rushing to do. List the items on the board, and let volunteers underline the digraphs in the word list (<u>sh</u>ut, ba<u>th</u>, ma<u>th</u>, and so on).

Day 4

Apply the Skill

Independent/Partner

Have children sort their cards again. Then, as a class brainstorm other words that begin or end with *ch, sh, wh,* or *th.* Then have children turn to page 10 in their Word Study Notebook. Read aloud the directions. Have children work independently or with a partner to draw pictures and write words that begin or end with the consonant digraphs *ch, sh, wh,* or *th.*

Day 5

Complete the Sort

Whole Group/Independent

Paste in Place

Have children turn to page 9 in their Word Study Notebook. Encourage children to say the name of each picture and then sort the picture cards into four categories according to consonant digraph *(ch, sh, wh, th)*. Then have them paste the pictures in the correct column on the page.

Play the Game

When children are finished, they may play Digraph Dilemma. (See the Teacher Resource CD for game board, playing cards, and directions.)

Building Vocabulary

If possible, show pictures or specimens of a moth and a butterfly. Explain that, in general, moths have fuzzy bodies and feathery or thin antennae while butterflies have smooth bodies and antennae with club-like tips. Also, moths are usually more active at night while butterflies are more active during the day.

ESL/ELL English Language Learners

Review with children the picture cards, naming each picture. Be sure that children are pronouncing each of the consonant digraphs correctly. For practice, have children use the words to create sentences that their classmates can identify as true or false. For example, a child can say "Wheat grows in ponds." (false)

Teacher Tip

You can extend learning by asking children to identify consonant digraphs throughout the day. For example, if the class is studying oceans, have children name ocean words containing *sh. (fish, shark, shell, ship, jellyfish, shore)*

Short and Long Vowel a

Objectives:

- To identify short and long vowel *a* sounds
- To identify and sort pictures and words that contain short or long vowel *a* sounds

Materials

 Big Book of Rhymes, Level B, "Twin Mix-Up," page 9

 Teacher Resource CD, Level B, Sort 3

 Word Study Notebook, Level B, pages 11–14

 Words Their Way Library, Level B, *The Name Is the Same*

 Teacher Resource CD, Level B, Around the Playground

Pictures/Words

long a	short a
frame	bag
snake	map
rain	bat
crane	jack
skate	ram
train	crab

Day 1 — Introduce the Sort

Whole Group

 Read a Rhyme: "Twin Mix-Up"

Read the poem "Twin Mix-Up" to children. Review the sound of short *a* and long *a*. Point to various words in the poem, or write the words on the board one at a time. Ask children if the word has a short *a*, long *a*, or neither. Explain that if the word has neither sound it is called an oddball.

 Introduce Picture/Word Sort Short and Long Vowel a

Print out and cut apart the picture and word cards for Sort 3 from the Teacher Resource CD. Show the cards to children as you name each picture. Define in context picture names that may be unfamiliar to children, such as *jack*, *crane*, *ram*, and *crab*. Start to show children how to sort the cards according to short *a* and long *a*. Encourage children to help complete the sort, then name each picture in the short *a* column and tell how the picture names are alike and different. Invite children to match each word to its picture. Continue with the long *a* column.

Day 2 — Practice the Sort

Whole Group/Partner/Independent

 You may want to begin Days 2–5 by reading the rhyme from Day 1. Then review the previous day's sort demonstration. Then help children tear out page 11 from their Word Study Notebook and cut apart the cards.

Have children work independently or with a partner to say the name of each picture and then sort the picture cards into two piles: short *a*, and long *a*. Then ask students to match each word to its picture.

Alternative Sort: Trip to the Zoo

When children have completed this week's sort, suggest that they pretend they are taking a trip to the zoo. Have children re-sort the cards so that one pile of cards shows pictures of animals that children might see at the zoo. The remaining cards should go into a second pile. If you wish, let a volunteer show the cards with zoo animals and describe the imaginary zoo trip.

Day 3 Find Words in Context

Whole Group

Have children re-sort their cards. Read *The Name Is the Same* to children. Ask children to help Coach Dan by thinking of a plan that would work. Divide the class into two "baseball teams," a short *a* team and a long *a* team. Appoint a scorekeeper for each team. Read the book again as the short *a* team identifies short *a* words and the long *a* team identifies long *a* words. Have the scorekeepers keep score on the board, awarding one point per word.

Day 4 Apply the Skill

Independent/Partner

Have children sort their cards again. Have the class brainstorm other words with the short *a* and long *a* vowel sound. Then have children turn to page 14 in their Word Study Notebook. Read aloud the directions, and have children work independently or with a partner to write and illustrate short *a* words and long *a* words.

Day 5 Complete the Sort

Whole Group/Independent

Paste in Place

Have children turn to page 13 in their Word Study Notebook. Encourage children to sort the picture cards into two piles. They should make separate piles for short *a* words and long *a* words. Then have them paste the pictures and words in the correct column on the page.

Play the Game

When children are finished, they may play Around the Playground. (See the Teacher Resource CD for the game board, playing cards, word list, spinner, and directions.)

Building Vocabulary

Tell children that some words have more than one meaning. Ask if anyone knows what a *crane* is. Explain that a crane is a wading bird which has long legs and neck. It is also a machine used to lift and carry heavy objects. Tell children that the word *crane* can be an action word, too. Explain that *crane* means "to stretch one's neck to see better."

ESL/ELL English Language Learners

Review with children the picture cards, naming each picture. Have children pronounce the words after you. Then, using cards from two card sets, hold up two of the same picture (two snakes, for example). Help children practice pronouncing the plural of the word. *(snakes)* Continue with other card pairs.

Teacher Tip

When children work together in pairs, suggest that they take turns being the "teacher." It is the teacher's responsibility to check the work of the other child and help the child understand how to correctly sort the cards.

Sort 4

Short and Long Vowel i

Objectives:

- To identify short and long vowel *i* sounds
- To identify and sort pictures and words that contain short or long vowel *i* sounds

Materials

Big Book of Rhymes, Level B, "Things to Do," page 11

Teacher Resource CD, Level B, Sort 4

Word Study Notebook, Level B, pages 15–18

Words Their Way Library, Level B, *Dive In!*

Teacher Resource CD, Level B, Swim Time

Pictures/Words

long i	short i
slide	chin
smile	zip
dive	hill
write	crib
bike	pig
kite	twins

Day 1 Introduce the Sort

Whole Group

Read a Rhyme: "Things to Do"

Introduce short *i* and long *i* words by reading the poem "Things to Do" to children. Make two columns on the board, one for short *i* and one for long *i*. Have volunteers locate *i* words in the poem (*will, think, swim, in, rink, ride, bike, climb, if, with*), pronounce them, and write them in the correct columns on the board. If you wish, let children brainstorm other words for the lists.

Introduce Picture/Word Sort Short and Long Vowel *i*

Print out and cut apart the picture/word cards for Sort 4 from the Teacher Resource CD. Name the pictures as you show the cards to children. Demonstrate how to sort the cards into columns short *i* and long *i*. Ask a volunteer to name each picture in the short *i* column, tell how the words are alike, and think of another word that belongs in the column. Continue in a similar way with the long *i* column. Then invite children to match the words to the pictures.

Day 2 Practice the Sort

Whole Group/Partner/Independent

You may want to begin Days 2–5 by reading the rhyme from Day 1. Then review the previous day's sort demonstration. Then help children tear out page 15 from their Word Study Notebook and cut apart the cards.

Have children work independently or with a partner to say the name of each picture and, using the grid on page 17 of their Word Study Notebook, sort the picture cards into two piles: short *i* and long *i*. Then have children match the words to their pictures.

Alternative Sort: Silent *E*

When children have finished this week's sort, explain that a "silent e" at the end of a word can be a signal that the *i* (or other vowel) in the word will be long. Have children re-sort the cards according to whether or not the word ends with a "silent e."

Day 3

Find Words in Context

Whole Group

Have children re-sort their cards. Show children the cover of *Dive In!* Ask children to identify the long *i* word in the title *(dive)* and the short *i* word *(in)*. Read the story. Then go back through the book, page by page, and have children identify the short *i* and long *i* words on each page.

Day 4

Apply the Skill

Independent/Partner

Have children sort their cards again. Have the class brainstorm words with short and long *i*. Then have children turn to page 18 in their Word Study Notebook. Read aloud the directions. Have children work independently or with a partner to write and illustrate words with short and long *i*.

Day 5

Complete the Sort

Whole Group/Independent

Paste in Place

Have children turn to page 17 in their Word Study Notebook. Encourage children to sort the picture/word cards into two separate piles for short *i* words and long *i* words. Then have them paste the words and pictures in the correct column on the grid.

Play the Game

When children are finished, they may play Swim Time. (See the Teacher Resource CD for the game board, playing cards, and directions.)

Building Vocabulary

You may want to introduce other short and long *i* words, such as *mill* or *hive*. If children are unfamiliar with the word *mill*, explain that a mill grinds something into small pieces. Some children may have seen tabletop coffee mills that are used to grind up coffee beans or peppermills that grind up peppercorns into pepper. Other larger mills grind wheat into flour or corn into cornmeal.

ESL/ELL English Language Learners

Review with children the picture cards, naming each picture. Have children pronounce the words after you. Then let children practice pronunciation and sentence construction by asking each other yes/no questions. "Do you ever dive into a pool (fly a kite, ride a bike, sleep in a crib)?"

Teacher Tip

If a child is having trouble pronouncing a particular sound, watch the child's mouth to be sure his or her lips and tongue are positioned correctly.

Sort 5

Short and Long Vowel o

Objectives:

- To identify short and long vowel o sounds
- To identify and sort pictures and words that contain short or long vowel o sounds

Materials

 Big Book of Rhymes, Level B, "Where Is That Clock?" page 13

 Teacher Resource CD, Level B, Sort 5

 Word Study Notebook, Level B, pages 19–22

 Words Their Way Library, Level B, *When Bob Woke Up Late*

 Teacher Resource CD, Level B, Alarm Clock Race

Pictures/Words

long o	short o
nose	log
toe	sock
bone	top
goat	frog
coat	clock
hose	fox

Day 1 Introduce the Sort

Whole Group

 Read a Rhyme: "Where Is That Clock?"

Read the poem "Where Is That Clock?" to children. As you read, emphasize words that contain short and long o *(tock, clock, woke, not, stop, phone, on, top, oh)*. Review short and long o sounds. Then read the poem again, and have volunteers point out short and long o words. Write the words in columns on the board.

 Introduce Picture/Word Sort Short and Long Vowel o

Print out and cut apart the picture/word cards for Sort 5 from the Teacher Resource CD. Show the cards and name each picture. Define in context picture names that may be unfamiliar to children, such as *hose* and *fox*. Demonstrate for children how to sort the pictures by short o and long o sounds. Ask a volunteer to name each picture in the short o column and identify the short o sound. Then ask children to match the words to the pictures. Continue in a similar way with the long o column.

Day 2 Practice the Sort

Whole Group/Partner/Independent

 You may want to begin Days 2–5 by reading the rhyme from Day 1. Then review the previous day's sort demonstration. Then help children tear out page 19 from their Word Study Notebook and cut apart the cards.

Have children work independently or with a partner to say the name of each picture and, using the grid on page 21 of their Word Study Notebook, sort the picture cards into two piles: short o and long o. Then have children sort the words into the two piles.

Alternative Sort: Body Language

When children have finished this week's sort, ask them to re-sort the cards into two piles according to whether or not the card shows a picture of a part of the body. Point out that the piles will not necessarily be similar in size.

32

Day
3 Find Words in Context

Whole Group

Have children re-sort their cards. Read *When Bob Woke Up* Late with children. Turn to the longest note in the story (page 14 of the book). Point to the *o* words, one at a time, beginning with the word *clock*. Pronounce the word, and ask children if the word has a short *o* sound or a long *o* sound.

Day
4 Apply the Skill

Independent/Partner

Have children sort their cards again. Ask the class to brainstorm words with short and long *o*. Then have children turn to page 22 in their Word Study Notebook. Read aloud the directions. Have children work independently or with a partner to write and illustrate words with short or long *o*.

Day
5 Complete the Sort

Whole Group/Independent

Paste in Place

Have children turn to page 21 in their Word Study Notebook. Encourage children to sort the picture and word cards into two separate piles: short *o* words and long *o* words. Then have them paste the pictures in the correct column on the grid.

Play the Game

When children are finished, they may play Alarm Clock Race. (See the Teacher Resource CD for the game board, playing cards, spinner, and directions.)

Building Vocabulary

Write the word *fox* on the board. Ask volunteers to describe a fox. Explain that a fox is a member of the dog family. It has perky ears, a slender snout, a bushy tail, and reddish-brown or gray fur. Point out that in "The Gingerbread Man" and other stories, the fox is often a sly character.

ESL/ELL English Language Learners

Review with children the picture cards, naming each picture. Have children pronounce the words after you. Pass around a hand mirror so that children can see how their mouths form an *o* shape when they pronounce a long *o* word.

Teacher Tip

Remind children that they may come across *o* words that do not have the typical short *o* or long *o* sound. For example, the *o* in the word *shoe* combines with *e* to make a brand new sound.

Sort 6

Short and Long Vowel u

Objectives:

- To identify short and long vowel *u* sounds
- To identify and sort pictures and words that contain short or long vowel *u* sounds

Materials

 Big Book of Rhymes, Level B, "I Like Bugs!" page 15

 Teacher Resource CD, Level B, Sort 6

 Word Study Notebook, Level B, pages 23–26

 Words Their Way Library, Level B, *True or False?*

 Teacher Resource CD, Level B, Sound Match

Pictures/Words	
long u	*short u*
juice	run
fruit	thumb
cube	drum
tube	truck
glue	duck
tune	rug

Day 1 · Introduce the Sort

Whole Group

Read a Rhyme: "I Like Bugs!"

Read the poem "I Like Bugs!" to children. Ask children to raise their hand if they like bugs. Explain that you will read the poem again, and children who do like bugs should raise their hand when they hear a short *u* word. *(bugs, but, up)* The other children should raise their hand for long *u* words. *(true, cute, blue)* Read the poem again, and have children point out short and long *u* words. Write the words in columns on the board.

Introduce Picture/Word Sort Short and Long Vowel *u*

Print out and cut apart the picture/word cards for Sort 6 from the Teacher Resource CD. Name each picture as you introduce the cards. Define in context picture names that may be unfamiliar to children, such as *cube*, and *tune*. Start by showing children how to sort the cards into categories: short *u* and long *u*. Encourage children to help complete the sort. Have the class name each word and picture in the sort. Talk about how the words in each column are alike.

Day 2 · Practice the Sort

Whole Group/Partner/Independent

You may want to begin Days 2–5 by reading the rhyme from Day 1. Then review the previous day's sort demonstration. Then help children tear out page 23 from their Word Study Notebook and cut apart the cards.

Have children work independently or with a partner to say the name of each picture and, using the grid on page 25 of their Word Study Notebook, sort the picture cards into two piles: short *u* and long *u*. Then have children match each word card to the picture card.

Alternative Sort: Rhyming Words

Encourage children to further sort each column into words that rhyme *(cube, tube; truck, duck; thumb, drum.)* Help children understand that the words rhyme because they end with the same sound. Encourage children to name other words that rhyme the picture/word cards.

Day 3

Find Words in Context

Whole Group

Have children re-sort their cards. Read *True or False?* with children. Pause after each true/false question to allow children to predict the answer. Challenge children to identify three short *u* words *(buzz, bugs, run)* and five long *u* words *(true, glue, blue, use, clue)* in the book.

Day 4

Apply the Skill

Independent/Partner

Have children sort their cards again. Ask the class to brainstorm other words with short and long *u*. Then have children turn to page 26 in their Word Study Notebook. Read aloud the directions. Have children work independently or with a partner to write and illustrate words with short and long *u*.

Day 5

Complete the Sort

Whole Group/Independent

Paste in Place

Have children turn to page 25 in their Word Study Notebook. Encourage children to sort the picture/word cards into two separate categories: short *u* and long *u*. Then have them paste the pictures and words in the correct column on the grid.

Play the Game

When children are finished, they may play Sound Match. (See the Teacher Resource CD for the playing cards and directions.)

Building Vocabulary

Introduce other words, such as *suit* and *June*. Use a calendar to show that June is the sixth month of the year. Count the days in June, and locate Father's Day. Ask children with June birthdays to describe the usual weather during this month.

ESL/ELL English Language Learners

Review with children the picture cards, naming each picture. Have children pronounce the words after you. Children can practice vocabulary by naming words associated with each picture. Words associated with the fruit picture, for example, include *tree, seeds,* and *salad*.

Teacher Tip

Explain that *True of False?* contains true information. Tell children that books that contain true facts are called nonfiction. Fiction books contain made-up stories.

Sort 7

Short and Long Vowel e

Objectives:

- To identify short and long vowel *e* sounds
- To identify and sort pictures and words that contain short or long vowel *e* sounds

Materials

 Big Book of Rhymes, Level B, "Jean's Dream," page 17

 Teacher Resource CD, Level B, Sort 7

 Word Study Notebook, Level B, pages 27–30

 Words Their Way Library, Level B, *Steve's Room*

 Teacher Resource CD, Level B, Vowel Spin

Pictures/Words

long e	short e
feet	pen
jeans	desk
tree	web
beads	nest
dream	sled
leaf	ten

Day 1 — Introduce the Sort

Whole Group

 Read a Rhyme: "Jean's Dream"

Read the poem "Jean's Dream" to children. Review the sounds of short *e* and long *e*. Help children use sticky notes of one color to mark the short *e* words in the poem. *(ten, red, kept, them, bed, went, head, special, necklace, best, ever, when)* Then use sticky notes of a different color to mark the long *e* words. *(Jean, beads, she, near, sleep, seen, dream)*

 Introduce Picture/Word Sort Short and Long Vowel *e*

Print out and cut apart the picture/word cards for Sort 7 from the Teacher Resource CD. As you show the cards to children, name each picture. Define in context picture names that may be unfamiliar to children, such as *beads*. Start by demonstrating how to sort the cards into two categories: short *e* and long *e*. Then encourage children to help with the sort. Have the class name each picture or word in the column and discuss how the words are alike.

Day 2 — Practice the Sort

Whole Group/Partner/Independent

 You may want to begin Days 2–5 by reading the rhyme from Day 1. Then review the previous day's sort demonstration. Then help children tear out page 27 from their Word Study Notebook and cut apart the cards.

Have children work independently or with a partner to say the name of each picture and, using the grid on page 29 of their Word Study Notebook, sort the picture cards into two piles: short *e* and long *e*. Then have children match each word to the picture.

> **Alternative Sort: *t* or *n* Endings**
>
> When children have finished this week's sort, ask them to re-sort the picture cards according to the ending sound. Cards whose picture names end in *t* should go in one pile *(feet, nest)* and cards whose picture names end in *n* should go in a second pile. *(pen, ten)*. All other cards should go in a third pile.

Day 3 — Find Words in Context

Whole Group

Have children re-sort their cards. Read *Steve's Room* with children. Ask children to name the items Steve got to keep. *(shells, nests, jets, nets)* List the words on the board and have children identify the short *e* sounds. Then turn to pages 3–4, and challenge children to find two long *e* words. *(Steve, these)*

Day 4 — Apply the Skill

Independent/Partner

Have children sort their cards again. Ask the class to brainstorm words with short and long *e*. Then have children turn to page 30 in their *Word Study Notebook*. Read aloud the directions. Have children work independently or with a partner to write and illustrate words with short and long *e*.

Day 5 — Complete the Sort

Whole Group/Independent

Paste in Place

Have children turn to page 29 in their Word Study Notebook. Encourage students to sort the picture and word cards into two piles: short *e* and long *e*. Then have them paste the cards in the correct column on the grid.

Play the Game

When children are finished, they may play Vowel Spin. (See the Teacher Resource CD for the game cards, playing cards, spinner, and directions.)

Building Vocabulary

You may want to introduce other words with the short and long vowel *e*, such as *vest* and *peg*. If children are unfamiliar with the word *vest*, explain that a vest is a sleeveless garment, usually worn over a shirt. Children can make vests from paper grocery sacks. Hold the sack with the open side down. Cut two armholes and a neck hole. Slit the sack vertically down the front.

ESL/ELL English Language Learners

Review with children the picture cards, naming each picture. Then give one card to each child. Let children take turns describing their picture without showing it to the other children. Then have the other children try to guess what is on the card.

Teacher Tip

Over the past five weeks, children have worked with the vowels *a*, *e*, *i*, *o*, and *u*. You may want to check to see if each child knows the short and long vowel sounds. Sort 8 provides additional review of the long vowel sounds.

Sort 8

Review Long Vowels a, e, i, o, u

Objectives:

- To review long vowel sounds
- To identify and sort pictures and words with long vowel sounds

Materials

 Big Book of Rhymes, Level B, "My Summer Vacation," page 19

 Teacher Resource CD, Level B, Sort 8

 Word Study Notebook, Level B, pages 31–34

 Words Their Way Library, Level B, Summer at Cove Lake

 Teacher Resource CD, Level B, Vowel Sound Match

Pictures/Words

long a	long e	long i
cape	beak	bike
tape	cheese	dive

long o	long u
cone	tube
rope	cube

Challenge Words

shade	meal	spite
made	speed	slice
wove	mule	
stroke	use	

Day 1 Introduce the Sort

Whole Group

Read a Rhyme: "My Summer Vacation"

Read the poem "My Summer Vacation" to children. Ask children to name the five vowels they have studied (a, e, i, o, u) and to pronounce the long vowel sound of each. Have children look through the poem to identify words with long vowel sounds. (June, we, making, I, rode, train, own, hiked, over)

Introduce Picture/Word Sort Long Vowel Review

Print out and cut apart the picture/word cards for Sort 8 from the Teacher Resource CD. Introduce the pictures and words. Define in context words that may be unfamiliar to children, such as *beak* and *cape*. Demonstrate how to sort the pictures into five categories according to the long vowel sounds. Invite children to match each word to its picture. Have children name the words and vowel sound in the *a* column, and tell why the words belong in that column. Continue with other columns.

Day 2 Practice the Sort

Whole Group/Partner/Independent

 You may want to begin Days 2–5 by reading the rhyme from Day 1. Then review the previous day's sort demonstration. Then help children tear out page 31 from their Word Study Notebook and cut apart the word and cards.

Have children work independently or with a partner to say the name of each picture and, using the grid on page 33 of their Word Study Notebook, sort the picture cards into five piles according to long vowel sounds. Encourage children to say the long vowel sounds as they work. Then have children match each word card to its picture.

Alternative Sort: *Vacation Sort*

When children have finished this week's sort, ask them to pretend they are going on a trip. Have them sort the cards into two piles: items they would take on a trip or might do on a trip and items they would not take. Have children explain their choices.

Day 3

Find Words in Context

Whole Group

Have children re-sort their cards. Show children the cover of *Summer at Cove Lake.* Explain that the book contains letters written by Rose, the girl in the illustration. Read the book aloud. Then divide the class into eight teams, one for each of Rose's letters. Ask the teams to search their assigned letters for words with long vowels and report back to the class.

Day 4

Apply the Skill

Independent/Partner

Have children sort their cards again. Ask children to brainstorm other words with long vowel sounds. Then have children turn to page 34 in their Word Study Notebook. Read aloud the directions. Have children work independently or with a partner to identify the long vowel sounds in the words in the word box and then write the words under the corresponding vowels.

Day 5

Complete the Sort

Whole Group/Partner/Independent

Paste in Place

Have children turn to page 33 in their Word Study Notebook. Encourage children to say the name of each picture and then sort their pictures and words into five piles according to long vowel sounds. Then have them paste the pictures in the correct column of the grid.

Play the Game

When children are finished, let them play Vowel Sound Match. (See the Teacher Resource CD for the playing cards and directions.)

Building Vocabulary

To help children understand the word *cube,* show them a cube-shaped object, such as a six-sided die. Explain that a cube has six equal square sides. A shoebox has six sides, but it is not a cube because some of the sides are not square. Some items that are shaped more or less like cubes are referred to as cubes, such as ice cubes.

ESL/ELL English Language Learners

As you show the picture cards to children, name each picture. Ask children to take turns saying the words after you. This review lesson is a good opportunity to check children's pronunciation of the long vowel sounds.

Challenge Words Activity

Have children work with a partner to trace their right hand on drawing paper. Instruct children to think of a long *a* word and write it on the traced thumb. (If children need prompting, make suggestions from the Challenge Words list.)

Tell children to underline the letter *a* in the word. Then have children continue in a similar manner to write a word for each remaining vowel *(e, i, o, u)* on the remaining fingers.

Teacher Tip

This sort focuses on reviewing long vowel sounds. If you wish to also review short vowel sounds at this time, have children find short vowel words in the poem and in the story. In the Challenge Words Activity, have children trace both hands, one for long vowel words and one for short vowel words.

Final /k/ Sound Spelled -ck, -ke, or -k

Objectives:

- To identify various spellings of final /k/ sound
- To read, sort, and write words with final /k/ sound spelled -ck, -ke, or -k

Materials

 Big Book of Rhymes, Level B, "Jake Bakes," page 21

 Teacher Resource CD, Level B, Sort 9

 Word Study Notebook, Level B, pages 35–38

 Words Their Way Library, Level B, *How the Chick Tricked the Fox*

 Teacher Resource CD, Level B, Final /k/ Spin

Words

-ck	-ke	-k
pack	smoke	look
sock	woke	crook
lick	bake	hook
truck	like	book
lock	rake	cook
duck	bike	brook

Challenge Words

stack	brake	shook
brick	quake	took
quack	flake	nook
pluck	spike	

Day 1 Introduce the Sort

Whole Group

Read a Rhyme: "Jake Bakes"

Ask children to listen for words that end with the /k/ sound as you read the poem "Jake Bakes." When you have finished reading, have children name the words they heard. *(chick, Jake, snack, book, cake, cook)* List the words on the board and explain that a final /k/ sound can have different spellings. Ask children to count and identify the different spellings in the word list. *(three: -ck, -ke, -k)*

Introduce Word Sort Final /k/

Print out and cut apart the word cards for Sort 9 from the Teacher Resource CD. Introduce the words, and define in context any that may be unfamiliar to children, such as *crook, hook,* and *brook.* Demonstrate how to sort the word cards into three categories according to the spelling of the final /k/ sound (*-ck, -ke, -k*). Then have the class read the words in the first column and tell why these words belong in this column. (They all end in the *-ck* spelling.) Continue with the remaining columns.

Day 2 Practice the Sort

Whole Group/Partner/Independent

You may want to begin Days 2–5 by reading the rhyme from Day 1. Then review the previous day's sort demonstration. Then help children remove page 35 from their Word Study Notebook and cut apart the cards.

Have children work independently or with a partner to say the words and, using the grid on page 37 of their Word Study Notebook, sort the word cards according to the spelling of the final /k/ sound (*-ck, -ke, -k*).

Alternative Sort: Vowel Count

When children are comfortable with this week's sort, ask them to sort the cards according to the number of vowels in the word. You may want to review the vowel names before children begin. Children will make a pile for words with one vowel and a pile for words with two vowels.

Day 3 — Find Words in Context

Whole Group

Have children re-sort their cards. Read *How the Chick Tricked the Fox,* pausing after the third wish. Invite children to predict the ending. Review the different final /k/ sound spellings that children have been learning, and write them on the board *(-ck, -ke, -k).* Tell children that one of these spellings can be found throughout the book. Let children look through the pages of the book, and then ask which spelling they found. *(-ck)*

Day 4 — Apply the Skill

Independent/Partner

Have children sort their cards again. Ask children to brainstorm other words with final /k/ sounds. Then have children turn to page 38 in their Word Study Notebook. Read aloud the directions. Ask volunteers to identify the different /k/ spellings in the words *kick, take,* and *took.* Then have children work independently or with a partner to write words that rhyme with these three words.

Day 5 — Complete the Sort

Whole Group/Independent

Paste in Place

Have children turn to page 37 in their Word Study Notebook. Encourage children to sort the word cards according to the final /k/ sound spelling *(-ck, -ke, -k).* Then have them paste the words in the correct column on the grid.

Play the Game

When children are finished, they may play Final /k/ Spin. (See the Teacher Resource CD for the game cards, playing cards, spinner, and directions.)

Building Vocabulary

Suggest that children use context to determine the different meanings of the word *crook* in the following sentences. "I dusted every *crook* in the cabinet." *(curve, bend)* "A *crook* took the jewels." *(thief)* "The shepherd used his *crook* to rescue the lamb." *(hooked pole or staff)*

ESL/ELL English Language Learners

Review with children the word cards by having children repeat each word after you. Many of the words in this week's sort can be used either as nouns or as verbs. Have children use some of these words *(lock, pack, duck, rake, bike, cook)* in sentences.

Challenge Words Activity

Label three containers with the three /k/ sound spellings *(-ck, -ke,* and *-k).* Challenge the class to fill each container with words ending in these three /k/ sound spellings. Each child should think of and contribute one or more words per spelling, writing each word on an index card. (If children need prompting, make suggestions from the Challenge Words in this lesson.)

Teacher Tip

Some words in *How the Chick Tricked the Fox* contain the letters *ck,* but the letters are not at the end of the word. If you wish, point out these words and remove the endings to reveal words that end in the *-ck* spelling of /k/: *tricked, trick; licked, lick; chicken, chick.*

Spell Check 1

After completing sorts 1–9, you may want to administer Spell Check 1 in the Word Study Notebook on page 147. See pages 21–22 for instructions on progress monitoring and using the Spell Checks.

Short a (CVC) and Long a (CVCe and CVVC)

Objectives:

- To identify short *a* and long *a* vowel sounds
- To read, sort, and write words with a short *a* or long *a* spelling pattern

Materials

 Big Book of Rhymes, Level B, "Pancakes for Breakfast," page 23

 Teacher Resource CD, Level B, Sort 10

 Word Study Notebook, Level B, pages 39–42

 Words Their Way Library, Level B, *Pancakes!*

 Teacher Resource CD, Level B, Pancake Chase

Words

ă CVC	ā CVCe	ā CVVC	oddball
dash	frame	faint	said
camp	blame	train	want
stamp	snake	paint	
snack	crane	brain	
flash	place	main	
black	bake	snail	

Challenge Words

gasp	trace	waist
lamp	paste	bait
smash	waste	claim

Day 1 — Introduce the Sort

Whole Group

 Read a Rhyme: "Pancakes for Breakfast"

Read the poem "Pancakes for Breakfast" to children. Write the word *pan* on the board. Point out that *a* between two consonants (CVC) is often short. Now write the word *plate* on the board. Explain that the *a* in this word is long because of the silent e at the end (CVCe). Tell children that, in some words, the letters *ai* are used to spell the long *a* sound (CVVC). Have children identify other short and long *a* words in the poem (*can, stacks, dad, glad; makes, wait, made*).

 Introduce Word Sort Short and Long *a*

Print out and cut apart the word cards for Sort 10 from the Teacher Resource CD. Introduce the words, and define in context any that may be unfamiliar to children. Work with children to sort the words by the CVC, CVCe, and CVVC patterns. Place the words *want* and *said* in the oddball column. (They have neither short nor long *a* sounds.)

Day 2 — Practice the Sort

Whole Group/Partner/Independent

 You may want to begin Days 2–5 by reading the rhyme from Day 1. Then review the previous day's sort demonstration. Then help children tear out page 39 from their Word Study Notebook and cut apart the cards.

Have children work independently or with a partner to say the words and, using the grid on page 41 of their Word Study Notebook, sort the words into four piles: CVC (short *a*), CVCe (long *a*), CVVC (long *a*), and oddball. As children work, encourage them to listen for short or long *a* sounds as they pronounce each word.

Alternative Sort: /k/ Endings

When children are comfortable with this week's sort, ask them to re-sort the cards into groups of words that end with the /k/ sound (*snack, black, snake, bake*) and words that do not. Then review the words that end in /k/, and have children identify the -ck and -ke spellings that they learned in Sort 9.

Day 3 · Find Words in Context

Whole Group

Have children re-sort their cards. Read *Pancakes!* with children. Then divide the class into three groups. Have the first group identify the short *a* CVC words in the story (*man, fast, can, snack, stack, pan, batch, flap, catch*), the second group identify long *a* CVCe words (*make, table, plate*), and the third group identify the long *a* CVVC word (*wait*).

Day 4 · Apply the Skill

Independent/Partner

Have children sort their cards again. Ask children to brainstorm other words with short or long *a*. Then have children turn to page 42 in their Word Study Notebook. Read aloud the directions, and have children work independently or with a partner to write words with short or long *a*.

Day 5 · Complete the Sort

Whole Group/Independent

Paste in Place

Have children turn to page 41 in their Word Study Notebook. Encourage children to sort the words by vowel sounds and spelling patterns for short and long *a*. Then have them paste the words in the correct column on the grid. Remind children to paste words that do not have the short or long *a* sound in the oddball column.

Play the Game

When children are finished, they may play Pancake Chase. (See the Teacher Resource CD for the game board, Pancake Stack sheet, spinner, and directions.)

Building Vocabulary

If children are unfamiliar with the word *dash*, explain that a dash is a short, fast race. The word can also mean "to smash" and refers to the punctuation mark used in writing.

ESL/ELL English Language Learners

Review with children the word cards by having children repeat each word after you. To reinforce vocabulary, give each child a word card to illustrate on a separate sheet of paper. Show the illustrations, one at a time, and ask children to guess the words.

Challenge Words Activity

Provide tan construction paper, and invite children to cut apart "pancakes." Have children write a word with short or long *a* on each pancake. If children need prompting, make suggestions from the Challenge Words list. Work together to stack the pancakes in three piles: CVC (short *a*), CVCe (long *a*), CVVC (long *a*).

Teacher Tip

To help children remember to pronounce *ai* as long *a*, share the rhyme "When *a* and *i* go walking, the *a* does the talking." However, remind children that while this rule is true of other vowel pairs, there are many exceptions to this rule.

Short o (CVC) and Long o (CVCe and CVVC)

Objectives:

- To identify short o and long o vowel sounds
- To read, sort, and write words with a short o or long o spelling pattern

Materials

 Big Book of Rhymes, Level B, "Let's Go to Grandma's!," page 25

 Teacher Resource CD, Level B, Sort 11

 Word Study Notebook, Level B, pages 43–46

 Words Their Way Library, Level B, When I Go See Gram

 Teacher Resource CD, Level B, Going to Gram's

Words

ŏ CVC	ō CVCe	ō CVVC	oddball
clock	note	boat	love
crop	stone	float	none
cross	chose	coat	
shop	whole	toast	
lock	slope	soap	
knock	joke	toad	

Challenge Words

stop	cove	oak
drop	doze	croak
rock	smoke	groan
	stove	moat

Day 1 — Introduce the Sort

Whole Group

 ### Read a Rhyme: "Let's Go to Grandma's!"

Read the poem "Let's Go to Grandma's!" to children. Review the sound of short and long o. Ask children to listen for words with short and long o as you reread the poem. List the words in columns on the board, and have children identify different spelling patterns of short and long o: CVC (short o), CVCe (long o), CVVC (long o).

 ### Introduce Word Sort Short and Long o

Print out and cut apart the word cards for Sort 11 from the Teacher Resource CD. Introduce the words, and define in context any that may be unfamiliar to children, such as *chose, cross, crop,* and *slope.* Demonstrate for children how to sort the words by short and long o vowel sounds. Then have children help you sort the words by the following patterns: CVC (short o), CVCe (long o), and CVVC (long o). Have children read the words in each column and discuss how the words are alike. Notice that the oddball column header has been dropped. Have children look for the oddballs on their own.

Day 2 — Practice the Sort

Whole Group/Partner/Independent

 You may want to begin Days 2–5 by reading the rhyme from Day 1. Then review the previous day's sort demonstration. Then help children tear out page 43 from their Word Study Notebook and cut apart the cards.

Have children work independently or with a partner to say the words and, using the grid on page 45 of their Word Study Notebook, sort the cards into three piles by spelling patterns: CVC (short o), CVCe (long o), and CVVC (long o). Suggest that children listen for short and long o sounds as they work. Children can put words with no short and long o sound in an oddball pile.

Alternative Sort: Consonant Count

When children have finished this week's sort, have them re-sort the cards according to the number of consonants in the words. Children will need to make piles for words with two consonants, three consonants, and four consonants.

Find Words in Context

Whole Group/Partner

Have children re-sort their cards. Read *When I Go See Gram* with children. Then write the word *not* on the board. Have a child read the word and tell if the *o* is short or long. (short) Add a "silent e" to the word. Again, have a child read the word *(note)* and tell if the *o* is short or long. (long) Have children work with a partner to find and record four words in the story that have long *o* with silent *e*. *(home, robe, roses, hose)*

Apply the Skill

Independent/Partner

Have children sort their cards again. Brainstorm with the class other words with short or long *o*. Then have children turn to page 46 in their Word Study Notebook. Read aloud the directions, and encourage children to work independently or with a partner to write words with short or long *o* in each column.

Complete the Sort

Whole Group/Independent

Paste in Place

Have children turn to page 45 in their Word Study Notebook. Encourage children to say the name of each word and sort their cards by vowel sounds and spelling patterns for short and long *o*. Then have them paste the words in the correct column on the grid. Children can use the unlabeled column for oddballs.

Play the Game

When children are finished, they may play Going to Gram's. (See the Teacher Resource CD for the game board, spinner, and directions.)

Building Vocabulary

Explain that a *slope* is a piece of ground that is not flat. Other things can slope, too. To show various things with a slope, have children hold books, sheets of paper, or other items at a slant.

ESL/ELL English Language Learners

Review with children the word cards by having them repeat each word after you. When you get to the word *knock*, invite children to share knock-knock jokes. Knock-knock jokes provide the opportunity to practice intonation. For appropriate jokes, do an Internet search for "kids' knock-knock jokes."

Challenge Words Activity

Provide strips of colored paper, approximately 1 inch wide and 7 inches long. Have children write a word on each strip, using the various spellings of short and long *o*: CVC (short *o*), CVCe (long *o*), CVVC (long *o*). If children need prompting, make suggestions from the Challenge Words list. Then link the strips together to make three paper chains, one for each spelling.

Teacher Tip

Encourage children to add to the paper chains (Challenge Words Activity) throughout the week as they come across words with short and long *o*.

Sort 12

Short u (CVC) and Long u (CVCe and CVVC)

Objectives:

- To identify short *u* and long *u* vowel sounds
- To read, sort, and write words with a short *u* or long *u* spelling pattern

Materials

 Big Book of Rhymes, Level B, "Goodbye, Flu!," page 27

 Teacher Resource CD, Level B, Sort 12

 Word Study Notebook, Level B, pages 47–50

 Words Their Way Library, Level B, *The Doctor Has the Flu*

 Teacher Resource CD, Level B, One Card!

Words

ŭ CVC	ū CVCe	ūi CVVC	o͞o CVVC	oddball
bump	prune	bruise	bloom	build
skunk	cute	juice	moon	built
trust	flute	suit	tooth	
grunt	crude	cruise	spoon	
plus	mule		smooth	

Challenge Words

rust	mute	loop
fuss	fume	scoop
blush	fuse	loom
gust		booth

Day 1 — Introduce the Sort

Whole Group

Read a Rhyme: "Goodbye, Flu!"

Review with children the sounds of short and long *u*. As you read the poem entitled "Goodbye, Flu!," have children listen for words with the short *u* sound and the long *u* sound. List the words on the board in separate columns. Point out the different spellings of the long *u* sound. Help children identify an example of each spelling pattern: ŭCVC (such), ū CVCe (June), ūi CVVC (fruit), and o͞o CVVC (soon).

Introduce Word Sort Short and Long u

Print and cut apart the word cards for Sort 12 from the Teacher Resource CD. Introduce the words and define in context any that may be unfamiliar to children, such as *prune, mule, grunt, crude,* and *cruise*. With the class, demonstrate how to sort the words by short and long *u* vowel sounds. Then demonstrate how to sort the words by the following patterns: ŭCVC, ū CVCe, ūi CVVC, and o͞o CVVC. Put the oddball words *(build, built)* in a separate pile.

Day 2 — Practice the Sort

Whole Group/Partner/Independent

You may want to begin Days 2–5 by reading the rhyme from Day 1. Then review the previous day's sort demonstration. Then help children tear out page 47 from their Word Study Notebook and cut apart the cards.

Have children work independently or with a partner to say the words and, using the grid on page 49 of their Word Study Notebook, sort the words by short and long *u* spelling patterns. As children work, encourage them to listen for the vowel sound. Remind children to place any words without a *u* sound in a separate pile for "odd ones out."

Alternative Sort: Perfect Fit

Draw five small boxes on the board. When children are comfortable with this week's sort, have them re-sort the cards. Instruct children to make two piles, one pile for five-letter words (the words that would fit one letter perfectly into each of the five boxes) and one pile for the other words.

Day 3

Find Words in Context

Whole Group

Have children re-sort their cards. Read *The Doctor Has the Flu* with children. Leaf through the book as children act as "word detectives" to identify words with short and long *u* sounds. Point out that in the words *chew*, *stew*, and *new*, the long *u* sound is spelled *ew*. Test each of the words that children identify by saying the word aloud to hear the vowel sound. Then discuss the word's short or long *u* spelling.

Day 4

Apply the Skill

Independent/Partner

Have children sort their cards again. Have children brainstorm other words with short or long *u*. Then have children turn to page 50 in their Word Study Notebook. Read aloud the directions, and encourage children to work independently or with a partner to write words with short or long *u*.

Day 5

Complete the Sort

Whole Group/Independent

Paste in Place

Have children turn to page 49 in their Word Study Notebook. Invite children to sort their words by vowel sounds and spelling patterns for short and long *u*. Then have them paste the words in the correct column on the grid. Be sure children understand that the unlabeled column can be used for any oddballs.

Play the Game

When children are finished, they may play One Card! (See the Teacher Resource CD for the playing cards and directions.)

Building Vocabulary

Discuss the word *trust*. Explain that if you can count on someone to do what is right, you can trust that person. Name something you trust the children to do. For example, tell children you trust them to do their best on the word sorts.

ESL/ELL English Language Learners

Review the word cards with children by having them repeat each word after you. You may need to explain the meanings of the words *prune* (dried plum) and *mule* (donkey-like animal). Explain that the word *crude* can be used to describe impolite words (crude remark) or materials that are still in a rough state (crude woodwork, crude oil).

Challenge Words Activity

Have each child draw and cut apart a large four-leaf clover from green construction paper (or provide a paper pattern). Instruct children to write "Lucky U" on the stem and words on each of the four leaves, using the four spellings of short and long *u* (ŭ CVC, ū CVCe, ui CVVC, o͞o CVVC). If children need prompting to help them think of words, make suggestions from the Challenge Words list.

Teacher Tip

If some children are having difficulty sorting words with short *u* and long *u*, pair them with children who are more proficient.

Short e (CVC) and Long e (CVVC)

Objectives:

- To identify short *e* and long *e* vowel sounds
- To read, sort, and write words with a short *e* or long *e* spelling pattern

Materials

 Big Book of Rhymes, Level B, "Shopping," page 29

 Teacher Resource CD, Level B, Sort 13

 Word Study Notebook, Level B, pages 51–54

 Words Their Way Library, Level B, *Eve Shops*

 Teacher Resource CD, Level B, Shopping Spree

Words

ĕ CVC	ēe CVVC	ēa CVVC	oddball
vest	keep	team	been
next	sweep	heat	
when	jeep	wheat	
web	teeth	clean	
dress	sleep	weak	
west	week	leaf	

Challenge Words

stem	speech	least
pest	speed	deal
went	greed	meal
them	creep	treat

Introduce the Sort

Whole Group

Read a Rhyme: "Shopping"

Read the poem "Shopping" to children. Review the sounds of short and long *e*. Read the poem again, but this time instruct children to raise their hand high whenever they hear a long *e* and lower their hands whenever they hear a short *e*. Ask volunteers to find words in the poem that illustrate three spellings for short and long *e*: ĕ CVC (*spent*), ēe CVVC (*need, succeed*), and ēa CVVC (*beat*).

Introduce Word Sort Short and Long e

Print out and cut apart the word cards for Sort 13 from the Teacher Resource CD. Read each word, and define in context any that may be unfamiliar to children, such as *vest, wheat, weak,* and *web.* Demonstrate how to sort the words by short and long *e*. Then show children how to sort the words by the following spelling patterns: ĕ CVC, ēe CVVC, and ēa CVVC. Have children read each word. The word *been* does not fit the spelling/ pronunciation pattern. Put it in a separate pile for oddball.

Practice the Sort

Whole Group/Partner/Independent

You may want to begin Days 2–5 by reading the rhyme from Day 1. Then review the previous day's sort demonstration. Then help children tear out page 51 from their Word Study Notebook and cut apart the word cards.

Have children work independently or with a partner to say the words and, using the grid on page 53 of their Word Study Notebook, sort the words by short and long *e* spelling patterns. Suggest that children listen for short and long *e* as they work. Remind children that they will need a separate pile for oddballs.

Alternative Sort: Twin Letters

When children are comfortable with this week's sort, have them re-sort the cards by words with "twin" (double) consonants or vowels and words without twin consonants or vowels.

Find Words in Context

Whole Group

Have children re-sort their cards. Read *Eve Shops* with children. Review the short *e* sound, and challenge children to find every short *e* word in the book. *(Ken, went, get, help, rest, next, them, met, checkout, set, they)* Provide paper and pencils so that each child can make a list. When children are finished, go through the book together, one page at a time, so that children can check their lists. Discuss the CVC spellings of these words.

Apply the Skill

Independent/Partner

Have children sort their cards again. Ask children to brainstorm other words with the short or long *e* sounds. Then have children turn to page 54 in their Word Study Notebook. Read aloud the directions, and encourage children to work independently or with a partner to write words with short and long *e*.

Complete the Sort

Whole Group/Independent

Paste in Place

Have children turn to page 53 in their Word Study Notebook. Encourage children to sort their words by vowel sounds and spelling patterns for short and long *e*. Then have them paste the words in the correct column on the grid. The unlabeled column can be used for any oddballs.

Play the Game

When children have finished, let them play Shopping Spree. (See the Level B Teacher Resource CD for the playing cards, gift pieces, Shopping Cart sheet, and directions.)

Building Vocabulary

Write the words *week* and *weak* on the board, and ask volunteers to read the two words. Explain that homophones are words that sound alike, but have different spellings and different meanings. Review the definitions of *week* "seven days" and *weak* "not strong." Invite volunteers to identify another pair of long *e* words that sound alike but have different spellings and meanings (for example, *meet, meat*).

ESL/ELL English Language Learners

Review the words with children by having them repeat each word after you. Then create sentences for children to complete with words from the word cards, such as "Before you go to bed, be sure to brush your [teeth]." Or "You can travel north, south, east, or [west]." Let volunteers create similar sentences for classmates to complete.

Challenge Words Activity

On index cards, have children write and illustrate words that show different spellings of short and long *e* (ĕ CVC, ēe CVVC, ēa CVVC). If children need prompting to help them think of words, make suggestions from the Challenge Words list. Display the cards on a bulletin board or mount them in a photo album. Have children help you group the cards according to the various spelling patterns.

Teacher Tip

Children may notice spellings of short and long *e* that are not covered in this lesson. Tell them that next week they will continue the study of different spellings of long and short *e*.

More Short e (CVC and CVVC) and Long e (CVVC)

Objectives:

- To identify short e and long e vowel sounds
- To read, sort, and write words with a short e or long e spelling pattern

Materials

 Big Book of Rhymes, Level B, "Eagles Fly," page 31

 Teacher Resource CD, Level B, Sort 14

 Word Study Notebook, Level B, pages 55–58

 Words Their Way Library, Level B, An Eagle Flies High

 Teacher Resource CD, Level B, Eagle Race

Words

ĕ CVC	eᵃ CVC	eē CVVC	eᵃ CVVC	oddball
best	head	street	reach	great
desk	bread	queen	steam	
web	thread	sweet	bead	
next	breath	greed	dream	
sled	threat	sleep	beach	

Challenge Words

swept	health	beef	flea
shelf	read	geese	peak
help		breeze	leak
left		greet	leash

 Day 1 Introduce the Sort

Whole Group

 ### Read a Rhyme: "Eagles Fly"

Read the poem "Eagles Fly" with children. Tell children that this week they will be continuing their study of the spelling patterns for short and long e. Ask children to identify words from the poem with short e between two consonants. *(head, when)* Then have children name words in the poem that have a long e sound. *(see, eagle, breeze, trees)* Explain that children will find other spellings of short and long e as the week progresses.

 ### Introduce Word Sort Short and Long e

Print out and cut apart the word cards for Sort 14 from the Teacher Resource CD. Read each word, and define in context any that may be unfamiliar to children, such as *steam, greed,* and *threat.* Demonstrate how to sort the words by the following spelling patterns: ĕ CVC, eᵃ CVVC, eē CVVC, and eᵃ CVVC. Place the word *great* in a separate oddball column.

Day 2 Practice the Sort

Whole Group/Partner/Independent

 You may want to begin Days 2–5 by reading the rhyme from Day 1. Then review the previous day's sort demonstration. Then help children tear out page 55 from their Word Study Notebook and cut apart the word cards.

Have children work independently or with a partner to say the words and, using the grid on page 57 of their Word Study Notebook, sort the words by short and long e spelling patterns. Suggest that children listen for short and long e as they work. Remind children that one card will be an oddball (no long or short e sound).

Alternative Sort: Beginning Blends

When children have finished this week's sort, have them re-sort the cards by words that begin with letter blends and words that do not. *(sled, bread, thread, threat, breath, street, sweet, greed, sleep, steam, dream, great)*

Find Words in Context

Whole Group

Have children re-sort their cards. Read *An Eagle Flies High* with children. Turn to pages 6–7 in the book, and have children identify words that show various spellings of short and long *e:* ĕ CVC (open), ĕ CVC (seven), and ēē CVVC (feet). Then have children point out and name parts of the eagle pictured on these pages. List the words on the board, and discuss any that contain short or long *e* sounds, for example: *beak* (ēā CVVC), *head* (ĕā CVVC), and *neck* (ĕ CVC).

Apply the Skill

Independent/Partner

Have children sort their cards again. Ask children to brainstorm other words with short or long *e*. Then have children turn to page 58 in their Word Study Notebook. Read aloud the directions, and have children work independently or with a partner to write words with short and long *e*.

Complete the Sort

Whole Group/Independent

Paste in Place

Have children turn to page 57 in their Word Study Notebook. Encourage children to sort their cards by vowel sounds and spelling patterns for short and long *e*. Then have them paste the words in the correct column on the grid. Remind children to paste the word that is an oddball in the unlabeled column.

Play the Game

When children are finished, they may play Eagle Race. (See the Teacher Resource CD for the game board, playing cards, spinner, and directions.)

Building Vocabulary

If children are unfamiliar with the word *greed*, explain that greed is the desire to have a lot more money or possessions than are needed. Greedy people often take more than their share without thinking of the needs of others.

ESL/ELL English Language Learners

Review with children the word cards by having children repeat each word after you. As children say the words, watch children's mouths to make sure they are pronouncing the words clearly and correctly.

Challenge Words Activity

Have each child fold a paper plate in half vertically and then horizontally. Then instruct children to cut on the folds to make four wedges. Tell children to write a word on each of the four wedges, using four different spellings of short and long *e* (ĕ CVC, ĕā CVVC, ēē CVVC, ēā CVVC). If children need prompting, make suggestions from the Challenge Words list. Have children arrange their wedges into "pies" that contain four words with the same spelling of short and long *e*.

Teacher Tip

When decoding, children may not know how to pronounce an *ea* word. They may wonder if the vowel sound should be short (ĕā CVVC) or long (ēā CVVC). Suggest that children try both ways and then select the pronunciation that produces a real word.

Review CVVC Patterns ai, oa, ee, ea

Objectives:

- To review words with an *ai, oa, ee,* or *ea* vowel sound
- To read, sort, and write words with *ai, oa, ee,* or *ea*

Materials

Big Book of Rhymes, Level B, "A Bad Day," page 33

Teacher Resource CD, Level B, Sort 15

Word Study Notebook, Level B, pages 59–62

Words Their Way Library, Level B, *Pete's Bad Day*

Teacher Resource CD, Level B, Match the Category

Words

ai	oa	ee	ea
wait	throat	beet	beast
pail	coast	need	beach
train	coat	sheep	cream
grain	goat	wheel	seat
tail	toast	three	neat
bait	road	cheek	cheat

Challenge Words

rail	moan	sleep	pea
chain	load	teeth	feast
claim	croak	green	least
plain	coach		

Day 1 Introduce the Sort

Whole Group

Read a Rhyme: "A Bad Day"

Read the poem "A Bad Day" with children. Write "___ai___" on the board. Ask children to look through the poem and identify a CVVC word with *ai.* (pain) Have a volunteer fill in the blanks on the board to write the word *pain.* Continue in a similar manner with *oa (groaned), ee (feet),* and *ea (head, eat,* and *screamed).* In some cases, children will need to write two or three letters in the blanks.

Introduce Word Sort CVVC Patterns

Print out and cut apart the cards for Sort 15 from the Teacher Resource CD. Read each word, and define in context any that may be unfamiliar to children, such as *beet, beach, coast, grain,* and *bait.* Demonstrate how to sort the words into four columns: *ai, oa, ee,* and *ea.* Starting with the first column, have children read the words with you. Ask volunteers to explain how all the words in the column are alike (same set of vowels, same long vowel sound, same CVVC pattern) and how they are different (different beginning and ending consonants). Continue with the remaining columns.

Day 2 Practice the Sort

Whole Group/Partner/Independent

You may want to begin Days 2–5 by reading the rhyme from Day 1. Then review the previous day's sort demonstration. Then help children tear out page 59 from their Word Study Notebook and cut apart the word cards.

Have children work independently or with a partner to say the words and, using the grid on page 61 of their Word Study Notebook, sort the words by spelling patterns *ai, oa, ee,* and *ea.* Suggest that children listen for the long vowel sounds as they work.

Alternative Sort: Land of Oz Sort

Tell children about the author of *The Wonderful Wizard of Oz,* Frank L. Baum, who reportedly named Oz by using the letters *O-Z* from his lower file cabinet. Have children sort their cards alphabetically into two piles, one for words that begin with the letters *A–N* and one for words that begin with the letters *O–Z.*

Find Words in Context

Whole Group

Have children re-sort their cards. Read *Pete's Bad Day* with children. Then give each child a word card. Instruct children to identify the vowel pattern on the card *(ai, oa, ee, or ea)* and then look for words in the book with the same vowel pattern *(toast; feet, sheet, green; screamed, jeans, sneakers, please, seat, hear, scream)*. Discuss the words children find for each of the vowel patterns.

Apply the Skill

Independent/Partner

Have children sort their cards again. Ask children to brainstorm other words with the letters *ai, oa, ee,* or *ea*. Then have children turn to page 62 in their Word Study Notebook. Read aloud the directions, and encourage children to work independently or with a partner to write and illustrate CVVC words with the letters *ai, oa, ee,* or *ea*.

Complete the Sort

Whole Group/Independent

Paste in Place

Have children turn to page 61 in their Word Study Notebook. Encourage children to sort their word cards by vowel patterns *ai, oa, ee,* and *ea*. Then have them paste the cards in the correct column on the page.

Play the Game

When children are finished, they may play Match the Category. (See the Teacher Resource CD for the playing cards and directions.)

Building Vocabulary

To help children understand what the word *coast* means, explain that the land alongside the ocean is called a coast. It may be flat, sandy, steep, rocky, or icy. In contrast, a *beach* is a level stretch of sand or pebbles beside an ocean or a lake.

ESL/ELL English Language Learners

Review with children the cards by having them repeat each word after you. To practice language skills, give each child one or two cards, and have children create sentences using the words on their cards.

Challenge Words Activity

Provide old magazines and ask children to find words with the letters *ai, oa, ee,* or *ea*. If children cannot find words, suggest that they cut and combine letters from the magazines to create their own words. If children need prompting, make suggestions from the Challenge Words list. When everyone is finished, work together to sort the words into four piles, one for each of the spelling patterns.

Teacher Tip

Encourage children to add words to their sort piles (Challenge Words Activity) throughout the week as they come across words with CVVC patterns.

Spell Check 2

After completing Sorts 10–15, you may want to administer Spell Check 2 in the Word Study Notebook on page 148. See pages 21–22 for instructions on progress monitoring and using the Spell Checks.

Short a (CVC) and Long a (CVCe, CVVC-ai, and Open Syllable-ay)

Objectives:

- To identify short *a* and long *a* vowel sounds
- To read, sort, and write words with a short *a* or long *a* spelling pattern

Materials

 Big Book of Rhymes, Level B, "The Cat Chaser," page 35

 Teacher Resource CD, Level B, Sort 16

 Word Study Notebook, Level B, pages 63–66

 Words Their Way Library, Level B, *Who Has a Tail?*

 Teacher Resource CD, Level B, Animal Race

Words

ă CVC	ā CVCe	āi CVVC	āy CVV
class	blame	brain	clay
grass	brave	drain	gray
past	shade	gain	play
smash	shape	grain	stay
stand	taste	nail	stray
trash	wade	raise	tray

Challenge Words

grand	grave	faith	jay
brass	graze	stain	sway
task	slate	fail	ray
tramp	stale	praise	slay

 Day 1

Introduce the Sort

Whole Group

 Read a Rhyme: "The Cat Chaser"

Read the poem "The Cat Chaser" with children. Write the title of the poem on the board, and call attention to the short *a* in the word *cat* and the long *a* in the word *chaser*. Read the poem again, and ask children to listen for and name more short *a* words *(have, as, fast, bad, can, and, after, at, last)* and long *a* words *(a, named, Ray, Nate, way, chases, waits)*.

 Introduce Word Sort Short and Long a

Print out and cut apart the word cards for Sort 16 from the Teacher Resource CD. Introduce the words, and define in context any that may be unfamiliar to children, such as *blame, wade, gain, grain,* and *stray.* Help children to sort the words by the following spelling patterns: ăCVC, āCVCe, āi CVVC, and āy CVV. Tell children that a syllable or a one-syllable word that ends in a long vowel sound, such as *stray,* is called an open syllable. One way of labeling an open-syllable pattern is to label it a CV or CVV pattern, since the *y* acts as a vowel in these long *a* words. Have children read each word with you.

 Day 2

Practice the Sort

Whole Group/Independent/Partner

 You may want to begin Days 2–5 by reading the rhyme from Day 1. Then review the previous day's sort demonstration. Then have children tear out page 63 from their Word Study Notebook and cut apart the word cards.

Have children work independently or with a partner to say the words and, using the grid on page 65 of their Word Study Notebook, sort the cards by short and long *a* spelling patterns.

Alternative Sort: One Sound or Two?

When children are comfortable with this week's sort, lead them in another sorting activity. Tell children that some of this week's words, such as *class, brave, grain,* and *play,* begin with a consonant blend. Have children sort the words into two piles: words that begin with a consonant blend and words that do not.

Find Words in Context

Whole Group /Independent

Have children re-sort their cards. Read *Who Has a Tail?* with children. Have children listen for and identify any words with short or long *a*. Then have children look through their word cards to find the one that matches a word in the text. *(stay)* Then have them find other short *a* and long *a* words in the story. You may want to point out that some words in the text, such as *babies* and *raise,* do not fit any of the long *a* spelling patterns from this sort.

Apply the Skill

Independent/Partner

Have children sort their cards again. Then have children turn to page 66 in their Word Study Notebook. Read aloud the directions. Have children work independently or with a partner to say each word and write it in the box with the corresponding vowel sound and spelling pattern.

Complete the Sort

Whole Group/Independent

Paste in Place

Have children turn to page 65 in their Word Study Notebook. Encourage children to sort their words by vowel sounds and long *a* spelling patterns. Then have them paste the words in the correct column on the grid.

Play the Game

When children are finished, they may play Animal Race. (See the Teacher Resource CD for the game board, playing cards, and directions.)

Building Vocabulary

If children are unfamiliar with the word *wade,* take them on an imaginary trip to the beach, a lake, or a river. Have them pantomime rolling up their pant legs, dipping their toes in the water, then wading in the water.

ESL/ELL English Language Learners

Check children's pronunciation and understanding of the words. Make sure they can orally discriminate between the short *a* and the long *a* vowel sound. Explain that although there are different spelling patterns for the long *a* words, they all have the same vowel sound.

Challenge Words Activity

Ask children to think of other words with the short and long *a* spelling patterns. If children need prompting, make suggestions from the Challenge Words list. Then have children play Spelling Pattern Tic Tac Toe. Each player chooses a colored pencil or marker and a spelling pattern. Player 1 begins by writing a word from the chosen spelling pattern on the Tic Tac Toe board. Player 2 then writes a word from his or her chosen spelling pattern. Play continues until one player writes three words in a row across, down, or diagonally, or until all nine spaces on the board have been filled in.

Teacher Tip

When children complete a sort, remind them to read each word in a column and note its spelling pattern to check their work. Some students may find it helpful to trace each long *a* spelling pattern with a different color crayon or marker.

Short o (CVC) and Long o (CVCe, CVVC-oa, and Open Syllable-ow)

Objectives:

- To identify short o and long o vowel sounds
- To read, sort, and write words with a short o or long o spelling pattern

Materials

Big Book of Rhymes, Level B, "Follow the Wind," page 37

Teacher Resource CD, Level B, Sort 17

Word Study Notebook, Level B, pages 67–70

Words Their Way Library, Level B, *Wilbert Took a Walk*

Teacher Resource CD, Level B, One Card!

Words

ŏ CVC	ō CVCe	oa CVVC	ow CVV	oddball
chop	close	boat	blow	lose
drop	dome	coach	grow	gloss
long	globe	loaf	know	
shop	note	roam	slow	
	wrote	roast	throw	

Challenge Words

dock	sole	cloak	flow
prompt	pose	boast	glow
stomp	quote	coax	show
blond	zone	loan	stow

Day 1 — Introduce the Sort

Whole Group

Read a Rhyme: "Follow the Wind"

Read the poem "Follow the Wind" with children, emphasizing the end rhyme. Write *ow* and *oa* as column heads on the board, and write words from the poem in the appropriate column. Tell children they will learn more words with these spelling patterns and other long o patterns in this week's sort.

Introduce Word Sort Short and Long o

Print out and cut apart the word cards for Sort 17 from the Teacher Resource CD. Introduce the words, and define in context any that may be unfamiliar to children, such as *dome* and *loaf*. Work with children to sort the words by the target spelling patterns. Explain that a one-syllable word that ends with a long vowel sound, such as *slow*, is called an open syllable. Place words *lose* and *gloss* in the oddball category.

Day 2 — Practice the Sort

Whole Group/Independent/Partner

You may want to begin Days 2–5 by reading the rhyme from Day 1. Then review the previous day's sort demonstration. Then have children tear out page 67 from their Word Study Notebook and cut apart the word cards.

Have children work independently or with a partner to say the words and, using the grid on page 69 of their Word Study Notebook, sort the cards by vowel sounds and long o spelling patterns.

Alternative Sort: Rhyming Words

Encourage children to further sort each column into words that rhyme *(chop, drop; note, wrote; blow, grow, know, slow, throw)* and words that do not rhyme. Help children understand that all of the -ow words rhyme because the -ow spelling pattern comes at the end of the word.

Find Words in Context

Whole Group /Independent

Have children re-sort their cards. Read *Wilbert Took a Walk* with children. Have children listen for and identify any words with short *o* or long *o*. Have children look through their word cards to find the ones that match words in the text. *(blow, slow)* Ask them what the two words have in common. (They both end in *-ow*, and they rhyme.) Then have children find other short *o* and long *o* words in the story and note their spelling patterns. You may want to point out that some words in the text do not belong in any of the long *o* spelling patterns from the sort *(go, so, no, oh, opened, hold)*.

Apply the Skill

Independent/Partner

Have children sort their cards again. Then have them turn to page 70 in their Word Study Notebook. Read aloud the directions. Have children work independently or with a partner to say each word and write it in the box with the corresponding vowel sound and spelling pattern.

Complete the Sort

Whole Group/Independent

Paste in Place

Have children turn to page 69 in their Word Study Notebook. Encourage children to sort their words by vowel sounds and long *o* spelling patterns. Then have them paste the words in the correct columns on the grid.

Play the Game

When children are finished, they may play One Card! (See the Teacher Resource CD for the playing cards and directions.)

Building Vocabulary

Explain to children that a *dome* is a shape found on the top of some buildings. Show children a *globe*. Explain that it is a sphere. Tell children to imagine cutting the globe, or sphere, in half. The result would be a dome. Show children pictures of domes, for example the United States Capitol building.

ESL/ELL English Language Learners

Review with children short and long *o* vowel sounds. Then read aloud each word, and have children listen for the vowel sound. When children hear a word with the short *o* vowel sound, have them shrink down to the floor in a squatting position to make their bodies short. When they hear a word with a long *o* vowel sound, have them stretch tall to make their bodies long.

Challenge Words Activity

Have children sort the Challenge Words according to spelling patterns. Allow children to play a game in small groups. Using a small cube-shaped box, write a spelling pattern on each side. You can use a pattern more than once. Invite Player 1 to roll the "pattern die" and identify the spelling pattern. The child should then say and spell a Challenge Word with the corresponding spelling pattern. Another player then takes a turn.

Teacher Tip

Some children may benefit from completing the sort in two steps. First, encourage children to sort the word cards according to short *o* or long *o*. Then have them examine the spelling patterns in the sorted long *o* words and complete the sort.

Short u (CVC) and Long u (Open Syllable-ew and -ue)

Objectives:

- To identify short *u* and long *u* vowel sounds
- To read, sort, and write words with a short *u* or long *u* spelling pattern

Materials

Big Book of Rhymes, Level B, "Big Baby Sue," page 39

Teacher Resource CD, Level B, Sort 18

Word Study Notebook, Level B, pages 71–74

Words Their Way Library, Level B, *The World's Biggest Baby*

Teacher Resource CD, Level B, Match the Pattern

Words

ŭ CVC	ew̄ CVV	ūe CVV	oddball
brush	chew	sue	do
truck	drew	blue	truth
dump	few	clue	sew
junk	grew	flue	
plump	knew	glue	
trunk	stew	true	

Challenge Words

crumb	shrewd	hue
tusk	strewn	cruel
husk	whew	fuel
slump	brew	

Day 1 — Introduce the Sort

Whole Group

Read a Rhyme: "Big Baby Sue"

Read the poem "Big Baby Sue" with children and ask them to identify and name words that rhyme with *Sue. (knew, grew, true, do, to)* Write them on the board. Direct children's attention to the spelling patterns in the words. Then ask children to identify the vowel sound they hear in the word *much.* (short *u*)

Introduce Word Sort Short and Long *u*

Print out and cut apart the word cards for Sort 18 from the Teacher Resource CD. Introduce the words, and define in context words that may be unfamiliar to children, such as *sue, stew,* and *flue.* Help children to sort the words by the following spelling patterns: ŭCVC, ew̄ CVV, and ūe CVV. Read each word with children. Tell children that the *w* in *ew* acts like a vowel and has the open-syllable pattern. Point out that *do, truth,* and *sew* go in a separate oddball column.

Day 2 — Practice the Sort

Whole Group/Independent/Partner

You may want to begin Days 2–5 by reading the rhyme from Day 1. Then review the previous day's sort demonstration. Then help children tear out page 71 from their Word Study Notebook and cut apart the word cards.

Have children work independently or with a partner to say the words and, using the grid on page 73 of their Word Study Notebook, sort the cards by vowel sounds and long *u* spelling patterns.

Alternative Sort: Many Meanings

Have children sort the words according to the meaning of the words. Have them read each word and identify its meaning or meanings. Children should sort the cards by words that have one meaning *(know)* and words that have more than one meaning *(brush).*

Day 3 Find Words in Context

Whole Group /Independent

Have children re-sort their cards. Read *The World's Biggest Baby* with children. Have children listen for and identify any words with short or long *u*. Have children look through their word cards to find those that match words in the text. *(few, grew, blue, clue, true)* Ask children how the words are similar and how they are different. Then have children find other short and long *u* words in the story and note their spelling patterns. Point out that like the sort words *do* and *truth*, some long *u* words in the story have different spellings. *(you, huge, two)*

Day 4 Apply the Skill

Independent/Partner

Have children sort their cards again. Then have them turn to page 74 in their Word Study Notebook. Read aloud the directions. Have children work independently or with a partner to say each word and write it in the box with the corresponding vowel sound and spelling pattern.

Day 5 Complete the Sort

Whole Group/Independent/Partner

Paste in Place

Have children turn to page 73 in their Word Study Notebook. Encourage children to sort their words by vowel sounds and spelling patterns. Then have them paste the words in the correct column on the page. Remind children that they will have words that don't fit the spelling patterns in a fourth column.

Play the Game

When children are finished, they may play Match the Pattern. (See the Teacher Resource CD for the playing cards and directions.)

Building Vocabulary

Explain that a *flue* is a tube or opening that smoke or gas passes through. Point out that fireplaces must have a way to keep the smoke from the fire from going into a house. The flue is in the chimney and carries the smoke up and out of the house.

ESL/ELL English Language Learners

Have English language learners work with more proficient English speakers as they complete the sort. Encourage the English language learners to say each word with the more proficient speaker.

Challenge Words Activity

Ask children to name other words with the short and long *u* spelling patterns. If children need prompting, make suggestions from the Challenge Words list. Then have children use a blank grid to make word cards for these new words. Have children work independently or with a partner to sort the words into categories.

Teacher Tip

To help children discriminate between the short and long *u* sound, have them sort the cards in a different way. Give children a large cup and an empty cooking pot. Explain that the pot is for an imaginary stew. Emphasize the vowel sound in *stew*. Then tell children that the cup is for an imaginary drink. Emphasize the vowel sound in *cup*. Have children say each word in the sort and listen to the vowel sound. If the word has a short *u* vowel sound, children place it in the cup. If it has a long *u* vowel sound, children place it in the stew.

Short i (CVC) and Long i (CVCe, VCC-igh, and CV Open Syllable-y)

Objectives:

- To identify short and long *i* vowel sounds
- To read, sort, and write words with a short *i* or long *i* spelling pattern

Materials

Big Book of Rhymes, Level B, "Don't Cry," page 41

Teacher Resource CD, Level B, Sort 19

Word Study Notebook, Level B, pages 75–78

Words Their Way Library, Level B, *Pick Up Nick!*

Teacher Resource CD, Level B, Fly Away!

Words

ĭ CVC	ī CVCe	īgh VCC	y = ī CV
bliss	grime	bright	cry
grill	quite	fight	dry
grim	rise	high	shy
quit	twice	night	sky
whisk	white	sigh	try

Challenge Words

filth	crime	fright	sly
risk	prime	slight	why
swift	chime	thigh	fly
twist	spice		spry

Whole Group

Read a Rhyme: "Don't Cry"

Read "Don't Cry" with children, emphasizing the end rhymes. Read the poem again, omitting the last word in each line. Have children supply the word to complete each line of the poem. Write the rhyming pairs *cry, sky* and *mile, while* on the board. Have children identify the vowel sound and note the spelling pattern in each pair. Slowly read the poem again and ask children to identify and name other long *i* words. *(my, kite, high, smile, lights)* Repeat the exercise with short *i* words.

Introduce Word Sort Short and Long i

Print out and cut apart the word cards for Sort 19 from the Teacher Resource CD. Introduce the words, and define in context words that may be unfamiliar to children, such as *bliss, grim, whisk,* and *sigh.* Help children sort the words by the following spelling patterns: ĭ CVC, ī CVCe, īgh VCC, and y = ī CV. Ask children to describe how the words in each column are alike and how they are different.

Whole Group/Independent/Partner

You may want to begin Days 2–5 by reading the rhyme from Day 1. Then review the previous day's sort demonstration. Then help children tear out page 75 from their Word Study Notebook and cut apart the word cards.

Have children work independently or with a partner to say the words and, using the grid on page 77 of their Word Study Notebook, sort the cards by vowel sounds and long *i* spelling patterns.

Alternative Sort: Rhyme Time

When children feel comfortable with the week's sort, ask them to say each word and listen to rhyming words. Encourage children to sort the words according to words that end with /t/, words that rhyme *(bright, fight),* and words that do not. Encourage children to think of other words that rhyme with the words in the sort.

Find Words in Context

Whole Group / Independent

Have children re-sort their cards. Then have a volunteer read the title *Pick Up Nick!* Ask children which two words rhyme *(pick, Nick)* and what vowel sound they hear in these words (short *i*). Read the book with children. Have children listen for and identify any words with short *i* (little, him, if, with, it's, into, did, it) or long *i* (my, likes, cry, I, while, I'd, try, smile).

Have children look through their word cards to find two that match words in the text. *(cry, try.)* Ask why the words rhyme. (They both end with open syllable *y*.) Then have children find other short and long *i* words in the story and note their spelling patterns.

Day
4

Apply the Skill

Independent/Partner

Have children sort their cards again. Then have them turn to page 78 in their Word Study Notebook. Read aloud the directions. Have children work independently or with a partner to say each word and write it in the box with the corresponding vowel sound and spelling pattern.

Day
5

Complete the Sort

Whole Group/Independent

Paste in Place

Have children turn to page 77 in their Word Study Notebook. Invite children to sort their words by vowel sounds and long *i* spelling patterns. Then have them paste the words in the correct column on the grid.

Play the Game

When children are finished, they may play Fly Away! (See the Teacher Resource CD for the game cards, playing cards, word list, spinner, and directions.)

Building Vocabulary

Explain that *"sigh"* means to let out a deep breath. Tell children that people usually sigh when they are tired or when they are unhappy. Demonstrate a sigh, and have children mimic you. Then give different scenarios and tell children to sigh if it would be appropriate: You have just won a contest; you have been doing homework for two hours; you can't find your jacket.

ESL/ELL English Language Learners

To help children with letter-sound association, focus on one column of the sort at a time. Point to each word, read it, and have children repeat it after you. Then say a word at random. Have children locate the word, point to it, read the word, and identify the spelling pattern. Repeat with several words from the sort.

Challenge Words Activity

Ask children to name other words with a long or short *i* spelling pattern. If children need prompting, make suggestions from the Challenge Words list. Have children use a blank grid to make word cards for these new words. Then have children use the words to play a game of charades. A player draws a card and acts out the word. The player who correctly guesses and spells the word then takes a turn.

Teacher Tip

Give advanced children consonant letter cards, vowel letter cards, and cards with some of the spelling patterns learned so far *(oa, ow, ew, ue, igh)*. Invite children to use the cards to create words. Have them make a list of the words and see how many different words they can create.

Short i, o (CVCC) and Long i, o (VCC)

Objectives:

- To identify short *i*, long *i*, short *o*, and long *o* vowel sounds
- To read, sort, and write words with a short *i*, long *i*, short *o*, or long *o* spelling pattern

Materials

 Big Book of Rhymes, Level B, "A Wild Ride," page 43

 Teacher Resource CD, Level B, Sort 20

 Word Study Notebook, Level B, pages 79–82

 Words Their Way Library, Level B, *Grandpa, Grandma, and the Tractor*

 Teacher Resource CD, Level B, Grandpa's Farm

Words

ĭ CVCC	ī VCC	ŏ CVCC	ō VCC
fist	blind	fond	both
kiss	child	lost	cold
slick	find	moss	gold
will	kind	pond	most
wish	mild		roll
	mind		scold

Challenge Words

mint	wild	toss	host
hint	bind	cross	bolt
sift		floss	volt
tilt			comb

Day 1 Introduce the Sort

Whole Group

Read a Rhyme: "A Wild Ride"

To introduce the week's sort, read "A Wild Ride." Read the poem again, and have children identify words with short and long *i* and short and long *o*. Write the words in four columns on the board. Call attention to the short *i* and *o* words with the spelling pattern CVCC (*hills, across, pond*) and the long *i* and *o* words with the spelling pattern VCC (*wild, find, mind; told, cold, roll, most, don't*). Circle the spelling pattern in each word.

Introduce Word Sort Short and Long *i* and *o*

Print out and cut apart the word cards for Sort 20 from the Teacher Resource CD. Introduce the words, and define in context words that may be unfamiliar to children, such as *mild, fond, moss,* and *scold*. Then work with children to sort the words by short and long *i* and *o* vowel sounds. Read each word with the class. Ask children to describe how the words in each column are alike and how they are different.

Day 2 Practice the Sort

Whole Group/Independent/Partner

You may want to begin Days 2–5 by reading the rhyme from Day 1. Then review the previous day's sort demonstration. Then help children tear out page 79 from their Word Study Notebook and cut apart the word cards.

Have children work independently or with a partner to say the words and, using the grid on page 81 of their Word Study Notebook, sort the cards by vowel sound.

Alternative Sort: Last Letters

When children feel comfortable with the week's sort, invite them to sort the words by final letters. First, have children sort the words into three piles: words with final double consonants, words with final blends, and words with final digraphs. Then have children re-sort each category by specific final letters, such as words that end with *-ss* or words that end with *-nd*.

Day 3

Find Words in Context

Whole Group

Have children re-sort their cards. Read *Grandpa, Grandma, and the Tractor* with children. Have children listen for and identify any words with short *i* (*is, in, spring, big, into, winter, bigger, little*), long *i* (*driveway, time, by, I*), short *o* (*got, job, not, off*), and long *o* (*drove, stones, snow, rope, old, told*). Then have children look through their word cards to find the one that matches a word in the text. *(both)*

Day 4

Apply the Skill

Independent/Partner

Have children sort their cards again. Ask children to brainstorm other words with short or long *i* or *o*. Then have them turn to page 82 in their Word Study Notebook. Read aloud the directions. Have children work independently or with a partner to say each word and write it in the column with the corresponding vowel sound.

Day 5

Complete the Sort

Whole Group/Independent

Paste in Place

Have children turn to page 81 in their Word Study Notebook. Invite children to sort their words according to vowel sound. Then have them paste the words in the correct column on the page.

Play the Game

When children are finished, they may play Grandpa's Farm. (See the Teacher Resource CD for the game board, spinner, and directions.)

Building Vocabulary

Explain that *mild* is a describing word. It describes someone or something that is gentle or kind, not extreme or severe. Name various things, and have children identify whether each is mild or not mild. Some examples are a pet cat, a tiger, a lemon, a cracker, a raindrop, and a tornado.

ESL/ELL English Language Learners

After children have sorted their words, invite them to use a tape recorder to record themselves reading the words in each group. Encourage them to replay the tape, listening to the pronunciations of the vowel sound in each sorted group of words.

Challenge Words Activity

Ask children to name other words with the short *i* and long *i*, and short *o* and long *o* spelling patterns. If children need prompting, make suggestions from the Challenge Words list. Have children use a blank grid to make word cards for these new words and sort the words according to spelling patterns. Then have children choose a spelling pattern and create a book incorporating all the corresponding Challenge Words.

Teacher Tip

Offer advanced children additional challenges. After sorting the words, invite them to alphabetize the words in each group. Children may also enjoy using rhyming words from the sorted groups to create rhyming sentences, such as *I'm fond of the pond*.

Sort 21

Review Long Vowel Patterns

Objectives:

- To review long vowel sounds
- To read, sort, and write words with common long- vowel spelling patterns

Materials

 Big Book of Rhymes, Level B, "Five Goats in a Boat," page 45

 Teacher Resource CD, Level B, Sort 21

 Word Study Notebook, Level B, pages 83–86

 Words Their Way Library, Level B, *Erik and the Three Goats*

 Teacher Resource CD, Level B, Vowel Pattern Match

Words

CVCC	CVVC	CVCe	CV & CVV Open Syllable
blind	bleed	bride	crew
fold	jail	glide	crow
ghost	school	grave	drew
grind	sneak	scene	glow
light	soak	shone	fly
sold	steep	slave	way

Challenge Words

scold	dream	slide	slew
bright	sweep	grape	blow
fright	trail	prune	fry

Day 1 — Introduce the Sort

Whole Group

Read a Rhyme: "Five Goats in a Boat"

Read the poem "Five Goats in a Boat." Then write the headings *CVCC, CVVC, CVCe,* and *CV/CVV Open Syllable* on chart paper, and reread the poem, pausing after each long vowel word. Have children decide in which column, if any, the word belongs. Then write the word under the correct heading. Save the chart to use again on Day 3.

Introduce Word Sort Review Long Vowel Patterns

Print out and cut apart the word cards for Sort 21 from the Teacher Resource CD. Introduce the words, and define in context words that may be unfamiliar to children, such as *grind, steep, glide, scene,* and *crew.* Then help children to sort the words by *CVCC, CVVC, CVCe,* and *CV & CVV Open Syllable* spelling patterns. Ask children to describe how the words in each column are alike and how they are different.

Day 2 — Practice the Sort

Whole Group/Independent/Partner

You may want to begin Days 2–5 by reading the rhyme from Day 1. Then review the previous day's sort demonstration. Then help children tear out page 83 from their Word Study Notebook and cut apart the word cards.

Have children work independently or with a partner to say the words and, using the grid on page 85 of their Word Study Notebook, sort the cards by long vowel spelling patterns.

Alternative Sort: Name the Vowel

When children are ready for an additional challenge, invite them to sort the words according to long vowel sound—*a, e, i, o,* or *u.*

Day 3 — Find Words in Context

Whole Group

Have children re-sort their cards. Read *Erik and the Three Goats* with children. Have children listen for and identify the long vowel words. Write each long vowel word on the chart you began on Day 1. Note that some long vowel words do not belong in any category in the sort. You may want to include these words in a fifth oddball column.

Day 4 — Apply the Skill

Independent/Partner

Have children sort their cards again. Have the class brainstorm other words with the target vowel sound. Then have them turn to page 86 in their Word Study Notebook. Read aloud the directions. Have children work independently or with a partner to say each word and write it in the column with the corresponding vowel sound.

Day 5 — Complete the Sort

Whole Group/Independent

Paste in Place

Have children turn to page 85 in their Word Study Notebook. Encourage children to sort their words by spelling pattern. Then have them paste the words in the correct column on the grid.

Play the Game

When children are finished, they may play Vowel Pattern Match. (See the Teacher Resource CD for the playing cards and directions.)

Building Vocabulary

Explain that the words *seen* and *scene* sound the same but have different meanings. Remind children that the word *seen* is the past tense of *see*. Explain that a *scene* is a stage setting or a picture of a place. Encourage children to describe a beautiful *scene* that they have *seen*.

ESL/ELL English Language Learners

To encourage children to interact with the words, have them use the words to play a game of Memory. Write each word on an index card. Turn the cards facedown in rows of six. A player turns over two cards and studies the vowel pattern on each. If the vowel pattern is the same, the player keeps the match. If the vowel patterns are different, the player returns the cards to their original position. Encourage children to read aloud the words and to help each other.

Challenge Words Activity

Hold a spelling pattern spelling bee. Write a spelling pattern on the board and announce that all of the words will contain that spelling pattern. When all of the Challenge Words with that pattern have been used, erase the spelling pattern and repeat with another spelling pattern.

Teacher Tip

To help children recognize vowel patterns, have them write the words using different colors for the consonants and vowels.

Spell Check 3

After completing sorts 16–21, you may want to administer Spell Check 3 in the Word Study Notebook on page 149. See pages 21–22 for instructions on progress monitoring and using the Spell Checks.

r-Influenced Vowel Patterns ar, are, air

Objectives:

- To identify *r*-influenced vowel sounds
- To read, sort, and write words with *ar*, *are*, or *air*

Materials

 Big Book of Rhymes, Level B, "Scarecrow in the Garden" page 47

 Teacher Resource CD, Level B, Sort 22

 Word Study Notebook, Level B, pages 87–90

 Words Their Way Library, Level B, *The Not-So-Scary Scarecrow*

 Teacher Resource CD, Level B, Find the Scarecrow

Words

ar	are	air	oddball
dark	bare	chair	bear
harm	fare	fair	heart
shark	hare	lair	pear
sharp	square	pair	where
start	stare	stair	wear

Challenge Words

spark	glare	flair
harp	flare	
scar	snare	
arch	spare	

Introduce the Sort

Whole Group

 Read a Rhyme: "Scarecrow in the Garden"

As you read the poem "Scarecrow in the Garden," omit the last word from each line. Have children supply each end word, and write the poem's rhyming words on the board (*air, hair, stare, scare*). Underline the *air* in *air* and *hair* and the *are* in *stare* and *scare*.

Introduce Word Sort *r*-Influenced Vowel Patterns *ar*, *are*, *air*

 Print out and cut apart the word cards for Sort 22 from the Teacher Resource CD. Introduce the words, and define in context words that may be unfamiliar to children, such as *bare*, *lair*, and *fare*. Then demonstrate for children how to sort the words by *ar*, *are*, and *air* spelling patterns. Point out that five words do not fit the week's spelling patterns and go in a separate oddball column. Read down each list and ask children to describe how the words in each column are alike and how they are different.

Practice the Sort

Whole Group/Independent/Partner

 You may want to begin Days 2–5 by reading the rhyme from Day 1. Then review the previous day's sort demonstration. Then help children tear out page 87 from their Word Study Notebook and cut apart the word cards.

Have children work independently or with a partner to say the words and, using the grid on page 89 of their Word Study Notebook, sort the cards by *r*-influenced vowel patterns.

> **Alternative Sort: Same Sound, Different Meaning**
>
> Invite children to sort the words into homophone pairs and words that are not homophones. Explain that many of the words in this week's sort are homophones, or words that sound the same but have different spellings and different meanings. (*bear, bare; fare, fair; stare, stair; pair, pear; where, wear*)

Day 3 — Find Words in Context

Whole Group/Independent/Partner

Have children re-sort their cards. Ask a volunteer to read the title *The Not-So-Scary Scarecrow*. Ask children which two words have *r*-influenced vowel patterns. *(scary, scarecrow)* Read the book with children, and have children listen for and identify any words with *r*-influenced vowel patterns. Point out that some words with more than one syllable, such as *garden*, may have an *r*-influenced vowel pattern in one syllable.

Have children look through their word cards to find two that match words in the text. *(hare, pair)* Then have children find other *r*-influenced words in the story.

Day 4 — Apply the Skill

Independent/Partner

Have children sort their cards again. Then have them turn to page 90 in their Word Study Notebook. Read aloud the directions. Have children work independently or with a partner to say each word, write its homophone on the line, and draw a picture of the new word.

Day 5 — Complete the Sort

Whole Group/Independent

Paste in Place

Have children turn to page 89 in their Word Study Notebook. Encourage children to sort their words by *r*-influenced vowel patterns. Then have them paste the words in the correct column on the page.

Play the Game

When children are finished, they may play Find the Scarecrow. (See the Teacher Resource CD for the game board, Scarecrow Map sheet, spinner, and directions.)

Building Vocabulary

Explain that a fare can be a fee you pay for transportation. Brainstorm with children a list of modes of transportation that usually require passengers to pay a fare (bus, train, airplane, and so on).

ESL/ELL English Language Learners

Place the cards with homophones faceup in pairs *(bare, bear; fare, fair; stare, stair; pair, pear; where, wear)*. Read each pair of words, and have children say them after you. Make sure children understand that the words sound the same. Point out that the words are spelled differently and have different meanings. Use each word in a sentence, such as "I have a pair of red shoes" and "The pear was very juicy." As you read, pick up the word card that goes with the sentence.

Challenge Words Activity

Ask children to find other words with *r*-influenced vowel patterns *ar*, *are*, and *air* in magazines or newspapers. Have students cut out the words and make a collage for each pattern. Encourage children to continue to add words to the collages as they come across them. If they are having difficulty finding words, allow them to cut out letters to create words, such as the words on the Challenge Words list.

Teacher Tip

Listen as children complete the sorting activities. Check their pronunciations and their ability to isolate and discriminate among the *r*-influenced vowel sounds in the sort. Regional dialects often show up in *r*-influences words. Help children find a sort that works for them. Provide individual guidance and reinforcement when necessary.

Sort 23

r-Influenced Vowel Patterns er, ear, eer

Objectives:

- To identify *r*-influenced vowel sounds
- To read, sort, and write words with *er*, *ear*, or *eer*

Materials

 Big Book of Rhymes, Level B, "Arctic Fox," page 49

 Teacher Resource CD, Level B, Sort 23

 Word Study Notebook, Level B, pages 91–94

 Words Their Way Library, Level B, *A Fox Lives Here*

 Teacher Resource CD, Level B, Word Create

Words

er	ear	eer	oddball
clerk	dear	deer	earth
fern	ear	jeer	heard
germ	fear	peer	learn
herd	rear	steer	
perch	spear		

Challenge Words

herb	sear	sneer	here
perk	hear	leer	yearn
stern	shear		

Day 1 — Introduce the Sort

Whole Group

 Read a Rhyme: "Arctic Fox"

To introduce the *r*-influenced spelling patterns in the sort, read "Arctic Fox." As you read the poem again, encourage children to join in. Write the words *clear, neat,* and *eerie* on the board. Read the words aloud, emphasizing the *r*-influenced vowel sound in each. Then circle the *r*-influenced vowel pattern in the words *(ear* in *clear* and *near* and *eer* in *eerie).* Repeat with *perch (er)* and *summer (er).*

 Introduce Word Sort *r*-Influenced Vowel Patterns *er, ear, eer*

Print out and cut apart the word cards for Sort 23 from the Teacher Resource CD. Introduce the words, and define in context words that may be unfamiliar to children, such as *clerk, herd,* and *jeer.* Help children to sort the words by *er, ear,* and *eer* spelling patterns. Read down each list. Explain that three words do not fit the week's spelling patterns and go in a separate column. These oddballs sound like words with the *r*-influenced *er* vowel pattern, as in *clerk,* but are spelled with *ear.*

Day 2 — Practice the Sort

Whole Group/Independent/Partner

 You may want to begin Days 2–5 by reading the rhyme from Day 1. Then review the previous day's sort demonstration. Then help children tear out page 91 from their Word Study Notebook and cut apart the word cards.

Have children work independently or with a partner to say the words and, using the grid on page 93 of their Word Study Notebook, sort the cards by *r*-influenced vowel patterns.

> **Alternative Sort: Noun or Verb**
>
> When children are comfortable with this week's sort, invite them to sort the words by nouns and verbs. Remind children that nouns are words that name a person, place, or thing, and verbs are action words. Lead children in a sort by reading a word and identifying it as a naming word or an action word. Point out that some of the words, such as *perch, steer,* and *spear,* can be both a naming word and an action word.

Day 3 Find Words in Context

Whole Group/Independent/Partner

Have children re-sort their cards. Read *A Fox Lives Here* with children. Have children listen for and identify any words with *r*-influenced vowel sounds.

Have children look through their word cards to find a word that matches a word in the text. *(ears)* Then have children find other *r*-influenced words in the story. You may want to point out the word *here* and note that although it has the same vowel sound as *dear*, it has a different spelling pattern.

Day 4 Apply the Skill

Independent/Partner

Have children sort their cards again. Then have them turn to page 94 in their Word Study Notebook. Read aloud the directions and the word in each column. Then have children work independently or with a partner to say the word in each column and write words with the same vowel pattern. Explain that children may use words from the sort or their own words.

Day 5 Complete the Sort

Whole Group/Independent

Paste in Place

Have children turn to page 93 in their Word Study Notebook. Encourage children to sort their words by *r*-influenced vowel patterns. Then have them paste the words in the correct column on the grid.

Play the Game

When children are finished, they may play Word Create. (See the Teacher Resource CD for the game card/answer sheet and directions.)

Building Vocabulary

Explain that to *jeer* is to tease or make fun of someone. Incorporate the definition of the word into a meaningful learning opportunity. Talk about the way a person feels when he or she is the object of another person's ridiculing, or jeering.

ESL/ELL English Language Learners

Make sure children understand the difference between the sound of *er* as in *clerk* and the sound of *ear* and *eer* as in *dear* and *deer*. Help them with the pronunciation of the different sounds, pointing out the difference in mouth position. Suggest children use a handheld mirror to help them with their enunciation.

Challenge Words Activity

Ask children to name other words with *r*-influenced vowel patterns *er*, *ear*, and *eer*. If children need prompting, make suggestions from the Challenge Words list. Then have children make a flower for each spelling pattern of the sort. Have children write the vowel pattern in the center of the flower and a Challenge Word on each petal that corresponds to that flower's spelling pattern.

Teacher Tip

Invite children to implement what they have learned about *r*-influenced vowel patterns from this week's sort. Encourage them to create ten fill-in-the-blank sentences. Each sentence's missing word should be a word from this week's sort. Children should exchange sentences with a partner and complete the sentences, spelling the missing word based on their knowledge of *r*-influenced vowel patterns.

r-Influenced Vowel Patterns ir, ire, ier

Objectives:

- To identify *r*-influenced vowel sounds
- To read, sort, and write words with *ir*, *ire*, or *ier*

Materials

 Big Book of Rhymes, Level B, "Shirelle at the Game," page 51

 Teacher Resource CD, Level B, Sort 24

 Word Study Notebook, Level B, pages 95–98

 Words Their Way Library, Level B, *Miss Muffet and the Spider*

 Teacher Resource CD, Level B, *Around the Bases*

Words

ir	ire	ier	oddball
birth	sire	crier	clerk
first	hire	flier	fur
girl	tire	pliers	her
shirt	umpire		purse
third	wire		

Challenge Words

firm	sire	frier	liar
sir	spire		
whir	mire		

Introduce the Sort

Whole Group

 Read a Rhyme: "Shirelle at the Game"

As you read the poem "Shirelle at the Game," omit the rhyming words at the end of every other line *(umpire, wire, higher, flier)*. Have children supply the rhyming words, and write them in a column on the board. Underline the *r*-influenced vowel pattern in each word. Also write the words *third* and *Shirelle* on the board. Underline the *ir* in each word.

 Introduce Word Sort *r*-Influenced Vowel Patterns *ir, ire, ier*

Print out and cut apart the word cards for Sort 24 from the Teacher Resource CD. Introduce the words, and define in context words that may be unfamiliar to children, such as *umpire, flier, sire,* and *pliers*. Help children sort the words by *ir, ire,* and *ier* spelling patterns. Read the word lists. Explain that four words do not fit the week's spelling patterns and go in a separate oddball column.

Practice the Sort

Whole Group/Independent/Partner

 You may want to begin Days 2–5 by reading the rhyme from Day 1. Then review the previous day's sort demonstration. Then help children tear out page 95 from their Word Study Notebook and cut apart the word cards.

Have children work independently or with a partner to say the words and, using the grid on page 97 of their Word Study Notebook, sort the cards by *r*-influenced vowel patterns.

> **Alternative Sort: Word Beats**
> When children are comfortable with this week's sort, invite them to sort the words by syllables. Review the meaning of *syllables* with children. Then read a word on a word card and clap the syllables as you do so *(birth,* one clap; *umpire,* two claps). Continue by sorting the cards into words with one syllable and words with two syllables.

Day 3 — Find Words in Context

Whole Group/Independent

Have children re-sort their cards. Read *Miss Muffett and the Spider* with children. Have children listen for and identify any words with *r*-influenced vowel patterns *ir* as in *birth (first, girl, sir, fir, thirsty, shirt)* and *ire* as in *hire (tire)*. Point out that some words with more than one syllable, such as *thirsty*, may have an *r*-influenced vowel sound in one syllable. Then have children look through their word cards to find words that match words in the text. *(girl, her, shirt, first)*

Day 4 — Apply the Skill

Independent/Partner

Have children sort their cards again. Then have them turn to page 98 in their Word Study Notebook. Read aloud the directions and the word in each column. Have children work independently or with a partner to say the word in each column and write words with the same vowel pattern. Explain that children may use words from the sort or words they think of on their own.

Day 5 — Complete the Sort

Whole Group/Independent

Paste in Place

Have children turn to page 97 in their Word Study Notebook. Invite children to sort their words by *r*-influenced vowel patterns. Then have them paste the words in the correct column on the page.

Play the Game

When children are finished, they may play Around the Bases. (See the Teacher Resource CD for the game board, playing cards, and directions.)

Building Vocabulary

Show children a flier from the mail or another source. Explain that one definition of *flier* is "a paper with an advertisement." Invite volunteers to describe fliers they have seen.

ESL/ELL English Language Learners

Make sure children understand the difference between the sound of *ir* as in *birth* and the sound of *ire* and *ier* as in *hire* and *crier*. Help them with the oral discrimination and pronunciation of the different sounds, pointing out the difference in mouth position.

Challenge Words Activity

Ask children to name other words with *r*-influenced vowel patterns *ir*, *ire*, and *ier*. If children need prompting, make suggestions from the Challenge Words list. Have children write each word on two cards. Then have pairs of children play Concentration with the Challenge Words.

Teacher Tip

To give children additional practice with the week's *r*-influenced vowel patterns, write words with *ir*, *ire*, and *ier* on index cards, placing a blank line in place of the *r*-influenced vowel pattern (*birth* is written as b____th). Encourage children to analyze each word to determine its pronunciation, then fill in the correct *r*-influenced vowel pattern.

r-Influenced Vowel Patterns or, ore, oar

Objectives:

- To identify *r*-influenced vowel sounds
- To read, sort, and write words with *or*, *ore*, *oar*, or *w+or*

Materials

 Big Book of Rhymes, Level B, "The Snoring Horse," page 53

 Teacher Resource CD, Level B, Sort 25

 Word Study Notebook, Level B, pages 99–102

 Words Their Way Library, Level B, *Friends Forever: A Tale About Lion and Mouse*

 Teacher Resource CD, Level B, Guess the Picture

Words

or	*ore*	*oar*	*w+or*	*oddball*
corn	more	boar	work	floor
fork	store	oar	world	four
horse	tore	roar	worm	poor
for	wore	soar	worse	
storm	sore	hoarse		

Challenge Words

chord	swore	coarse	word	court
ford	gorge		worst	fourth
sworn			worth	pour
forge				

Day 1

Introduce the Sort

Whole Group

 ### Read a Rhyme: "The Snoring Horse"

As you read the poem "The Snoring Horse," omit the final word in each line. Have children supply each end word, and write the rhyming words *(door, roar, anymore, store, more)* on the board. Circle *oar* in *roar*, and *ore* in *anymore, store,* and *more*. Point out that *door* has the same vowel sound but a different spelling pattern. Invite children to look for other words in the poem with *r*-influenced vowel patterns *or, ore,* or *oar*. *(horse, snoring, forever)*

 ### Introduce Word Sort *r*-Influenced Vowel Patterns *or, ore, oar*

Print out and cut apart the word cards for Sort 25 from the Teacher Resource CD. Introduce the words, and define in context words that may be unfamiliar to children, such as *boar, oar,* and *hoarse*. Help children sort the words into *or, ore, oar,* and *w+or* spelling patterns. Read down each list. Explain that three words do not fit the week's spelling patterns and go in a separate oddball column.

Day 2

Practice the Sort

Whole Group/Independent/Partner

 You may want to begin Days 2–5 by reading the rhyme from Day 1. Then review the previous day's sort demonstration. Then help children tear out page 99 from their Word Study Notebook and cut apart the word cards.

Have children work independently or with a partner to say the words and, using the grid on page 101 of the Word Study Notebook, sort the cards by spelling pattern.

Alternative Sort: Two-Part Sort

When children are comfortable with this week's sort, have children sort the words by naming words, action words, and describing words. Point out that some words, such as *work*, can be both a noun and a verb. Children should choose a meaning of the word and then sort the card accordingly.

Day 3

Find Words in Context

Whole Group/Independent/Partner

Have children re-sort their cards. Read *Friends Forever: A Tale About Lion and Mouse* with children. Have children listen for and identify any words with *r*-influenced vowel patterns *or* as in *corn*, *ore* as in *more*, and *oar* as in *roar*. Point out that some words with more than one syllable, such as *forever*, may have an *r*-influenced vowel sound in one syllable. Then have children look through their word cards to find the three words that match words in the text. *(more, tore, roar)*

Day 4

Apply the Skill

Independent/Partner

Have children sort their cards again. Then have them turn to page 102 in their Word Study Notebook. Read aloud the directions and the word in each column. Then have children work independently or with a partner to say the word in each column and write words with the same vowel pattern. Explain that they may use words from the sort or words they think of on their own.

Day 5

Complete the Sort

Whole Group/Independent

Paste in Place

Have children turn to page 101 in their Word Study Notebook. Invite children to sort their words by *r*-influenced vowel pattern. Then have them paste the words in the correct column on the page.

Play the Game

When children are finished, they may play Guess the Picture. (See the Teacher Resource CD for the playing cards and directions.)

Building Vocabulary

Point out the homophones *horse* and *hoarse*. Explain that *hoarse* is a describing word. It describes a voice that is low and strained. Describe scenarios that might give someone a hoarse voice (yelling at a ball game, and so on). Have children use the word by completing the following sentence: "I was hoarse when I [write on line]." Explain that children may describe something that really happened or make up an ending to the sentence.

ESL/ELL English Language Learners

To encourage more confident and less stressful pronunciations, allow English language learners to use a puppet as they complete the sort. You can also model strategies to help children read and spell words with *r*-influenced vowel patterns. By "thinking aloud," children will hear how a proficient English speaker reaches a conclusion regarding pronunciation and spelling.

Challenge Words Activity

Ask children to name other words with *r*-influenced vowel patterns *or*, *ore*, *oar*, and *w+or*. If children need prompting, make suggestions from the Challenge Words list. Then have children draw a picture of a store and label the shelves *or*, *ore*, *oar*, and *w+or*. Have children write Challenge Words on the corresponding shelves.

Teacher Tip

As children learn *r*-influenced vowel patterns, they will make errors as part of the learning process. Encourage a supportive classroom environment, helping more proficient children understand and appreciate the attempts and accomplishments of less proficient classmates.

r-Influenced Vowel Patterns   ur, ure, ur_e

Objectives:

- To identify words with *r*-influenced vowel sounds
- To read, sort, and write words with *ur, ure,* or *ur_e*

Materials

 Big Book of Rhymes, Level B, "Watching for Sea Turtles," page 55

 Teacher Resource CD, Level B, Sort 26

 Word Study Notebook, Level B, pages 103–106

 Words Their Way Library, Level B, *Sea Turtle Night*

 Teacher Resource CD, Level B, Sure Pairs

Words

ur	ure	ur_e
churn	lure	nurse
curb	injure	purse
surf	nature	splurge
burn	cure	curse
purple	pure	
hurt	future	

Challenge Words

blurt	feature	purge
lurch		
spurt		
burr		

Introduce the Sort

Whole Group

 Read a Rhyme: "Watching for Sea Turtles"

Introduce words with *r*-influenced vowel patterns by reading the poem "Watching for Sea Turtles." As you read, emphasize the words *turtles, curved, hurry,* and *surely.* Ask children to locate those words in the poem. Write the words on the board, and circle *ur* in *turtles, curved,* and *hurry,* and *ure* in *surely.* Then ask children how the words are alike. Read the poem again, omitting those words, and have children supply the missing words.

 Introduce Word Sort *r*-Influenced Vowel Patterns *ur, ure, ur_e*

Print and cut apart the word cards for Sort 26 from the Teacher Resource CD. Introduce the words, and define in context words that may be unfamiliar to children, such as *churn, lure, splurge,* and *curse.* Help children sort the words into *ur, ure,* and *ur_e* spelling patterns. Read down each list. Ask children how the words in each group are alike.

Practice the Sort

Whole Group/Independent/Partner

 You may want to begin Days 2–5 by reading the rhyme from Day 1. Then review the previous day's sort demonstration. Then help children tear out page 103 from their Word Study Notebook and cut apart the word cards.

Have children work independently or with a partner to say the words and, using the grid on page 105 of their Word Study Notebook, sort the words by spelling pattern.

Alternative Sort: Guess My Category

When children are comfortable with this week's sort, re-sort the words into groups of words that name things and words that do not name things. Begin by sorting two or three of the words into the categories. When you pick up the next word card, invite children to guess where it will go. Continue to do this until all the cards have been sorted and children are able to guess the categories.

3 Find Words in Context

Whole Group/Independent

Have children re-sort their cards. Read *Sea Turtle Night* with children. Have children listen for and identify any words that contain *r*-influenced vowel patterns. *(turns, turtle, sure, hurt, returns, burst, hurry)* Then have children look through their word cards to find a word that matches a word in the text *(hurt).*

Day

4 Apply the Skill

Independent/Partner

Have children sort their cards again. Ask children to brainstorm other words with the same spelling patterns as *turn, sure,* and *curve.* Then have them turn to page 106 in their Word Study Notebook. Read aloud the directions. Have children work independently or with a partner to write words with the same spelling patterns as *turn, sure,* and *curve.* Explain that they may use words from the sort or words they think of on their own.

Day

5 Complete the Sort

Whole Group/Independent

Paste in Place

Have children turn to page 105 in their Word Study Notebook. Encourage children to sort their words by *ur, ure,* and *ur_e* spelling patterns. Then have them paste the words in the correct column on the grid.

Play the Game

When children are finished, they may play Sure Pairs. (See the Teacher Resource CD for the playing cards and directions.)

Building Vocabulary

Tell children that *churn* means to turn or stir something very hard. Then explain that the word *churn* is often used to describe the process used to make cream or milk into butter.

ESL/ELL English Language Learners

Review the words with children. Explain that *surf* can be used as both a noun and a verb, and that *to splurge* means "to spend a lot of money on something." Have children pronounce each word to be sure they understand the similarities between words that contain *ur, ure,* and *ur_e.*

Challenge Words Activity

Ask children to name other words with *r*-influenced vowel patterns *ur, ure,* and *ur_e.* If children need prompting, make suggestions from the Challenge Words list. Then have children draw the outline of a purse and write the Challenge Words on it. Suggest that children circle the *r*-influenced vowel pattern in each word.

Teacher Tip

During a second or repeated sort, do not correct children when they place a word in the wrong column. Wait until they have completed the sort and have them read the words in each column to check them. If they still don't find the misplaced word, tell them what column it is in and have them find it.

Review of *ar*, Schwa Plus *r*, and *or*

Objectives:

- To review *r*-influenced vowel sounds
- To read, sort, and write words with *ar*, Schwa Plus *r*, or *or*

Materials

 Big Book of Rhymes, Level B, "Fern's Monsters," page 57

 Teacher Resource CD, Level B, Sort 27

 Word Study Notebook, Level B, pages 107–110

 Words Their Way Library, Level B, *The Monster Under the Bed*

 Teacher Resource CD, Level B, "R" Spin

Words

ar	*ər*	*or*
hard	earn	torn
card	nerve	score
yard	spur	snore
jar	search	snort
bar	pearl	bore
sharp	worth	horse
march	worst	chore

Challenge Words

arch	sir	force
scar	lurk	short

Day 1 — Introduce the Sort

Whole Group

Read a Rhyme: "Fern's Monsters"

As you read "Fern's Monsters," emphasize the words with *r*-influenced vowel sounds (*monsters, orchard, park, Fern, dark, under, her, large, store, forgets, more*). Ask children to locate those words in the poem. Then write these words on the board and ask children how the words are alike. Help them understand that these words all have vowel sounds that are influenced by the letter *r*.

Introduce Word Sort *ar*, Schwa Plus *r*, or

Print and cut apart the word cards for Sort 27 from the Teacher Resource CD. Introduce the words, and define in context words that may be unfamiliar to children, such as *sharp, nerve, spur, pearl, snort,* and *chore*. Then help children sort the words by sound pattern. Ask children to describe how the words in each group are alike.

Day 2 — Practice the Sort

Whole Group/Independent/Partner

You may want to begin Days 2–5 by reading the rhyme from Day 1. Then review the previous day's sort demonstration. Then help children tear out page 107 from their Word Study Notebook and cut apart the word cards.

Have children work independently or with a partner to say the words and, using the grid on page 109 of their Word Study Notebook, sort the words by spelling pattern.

Alternative Sort: Act It Out

When children are comfortable with this week's sort, have them sort the cards into words that can be used to describe actions and words that cannot. Children may enjoy acting out each action word.

Day 3
Find Words in Context

Whole Group/Independent

Have children re-sort their cards. Read *The Monster Under the Bed* with children. Have children listen for and identify any words that contain *r*-influenced vowel patterns. *(stories, monsters, Morris, fur, purple, ears, large, dark, turn, yard, car, under, where, horrible, barked, far)* Have children look through their cards to find a word that matches a word in the text. *(yard)*

Day 4
Apply the Skill

Independent/Partner

Have children sort their cards again. Ask children to brainstorm other words with the target *r*-influenced vowel sounds. Then have them turn to page 110 in their Word Study Notebook. Read aloud the directions. Have children work independently or with a partner to say each word aloud and write the word in the box that shows its *r*-influenced vowel sound.

Day 5
Complete the Sort

Whole Group/Independent

Paste in Place

Have children turn to page 109 in their Word Study Notebook. Encourage children to sort their words according to *ar*, *ər*, and *or* spelling patterns. Then have them paste the words in the correct column on the grid.

Play the Game

When children are finished, they may play "R" Spin. (See the Teacher Resource CD for the game cards, playing cards, spinner, and directions.)

Building Vocabulary

Review two meanings of the word *bore*. Tell children that *bore* means to make a hole in or through something. For example, a drill will bore a hole in a piece of wood. But *bore* can also mean dull or uninteresting. Challenge children to use *bore* in two different sentences.

ESL/ELL English Language Learners

Review the words with children. You may need to explain that *spur* can be used as a noun or a verb. Explain that when used as a noun, a *spur* describes the sharp wheel attached to a boot heel that a rider uses to urge on a horse. Used as a verb, *spur* means "to move to action." You may then discuss other words in the sort that can be used both to describe actions and to name things.

Challenge Words Activity

Ask children to name other words that contain *r*-influenced vowel patterns. If children need prompting, make suggestions from the Challenge Words list. Then have children use a blank grid to make word cards for these new words. Have children color code the *r*-influenced spelling patterns.

Teacher Tip

Encourage children to develop their own criteria for completing the sort. This exercise should be used to encourage children to find new and unexpected meanings and rules underlying their organization of the words.

✓ Spell Check 4

After completing sorts 22–27, you may want to administer Spell Check 4 in the Word Study Notebook on page 150. See pages 21–22 for instructions on progress monitoring and using the Spell Checks.

Sort 28

Diphthongs oi, oy

Objectives:

- To identify *oi* and *oy* vowel sounds
- To read, sort, and write words with sounds spelled *oi* or *oy*

Materials

 Big Book of Rhymes, Level B, "Digging for Treasure," page 59

 Teacher Resource CD, Level B, Sort 28

 Word Study Notebook, Level B, pages 111–114

 Words Their Way Library, Level B, *What Joy Found*

 Teacher Resource CD, Level B, Treasure Hunt

Words

oi	oy
join	soy
soil	joy
coin	decoy
moist	ploy
coil	annoy
boil	coy
broil	Roy
spoil	enjoy
oil	toy
foil	Troy

Challenge Words

noise	employ
choice	destroy
voice	

Day 1 Introduce the Sort

Whole Group

Read a Rhyme: "Digging for Treasure"

Introduce words with *oi* or *oy* sounds by reading the poem "Digging for Treasure." As you read, emphasize the words that contain *oy* or *oi* sounds *(coins, soil, enjoy)*. Ask children to locate these words in the poem. Write these words in a column on the board. Ask children why you should move one of the words into a second column. (The word *soil* has a different spelling for the sound.) Invite children to think of other words to write in each column.

Introduce Word Sort Diphthongs *oi, oy*

Print out and cut apart the word cards for Sort 28 from the Teacher Resource CD. Introduce the words, and define in context words that may be unfamiliar to children, such as *soil, moist, coil, soy, decoy, ploy, Troy,* and *coy*. Then demonstrate for children how to sort the words by *oi* and *oy* diphthongs. Read each list with children. Ask children to describe how the words in each group are alike.

Day 2 Practice the Sort

Whole Group/Independent/Partner

You may want to begin Days 2–5 by reading the rhyme from Day 1. Then review the previous day's sort demonstration. Then help children tear out page 111 from their Word Study Notebook and cut apart the word cards.

Have children work independently or with a partner to say the words and, using the grid on page 113 of their Word Study Notebook, sort the words by sounds spelled with *oi* or *oy*.

Alternative Sort: Student-Centered Sorts

When children are comfortable with this week's sort, have them work with a partner to devise their own categories into which to re-sort the words. Once they have established their categories, have them complete the re-sort.

78

Day 3 — Find Words in Context

Whole Group/Independent/Partner

Have children re-sort their cards. Read *What Joy Found* with children. Have children listen for and identify any words with the same vowel sound as *Joy*. *(noise, soil, coin, toy, joined, pointed, boy, Roy, choice)* Then have children look through their word cards to find words that match words in the text. *(Joy, soil, coin, toy, Roy)*

Day 4 — Apply the Skill

Independent/Partner

Have children sort their cards again. Ask children to brainstorm other words with *oi* or *oy*. Then have them turn to page 114 in their Word Study Notebook. Read aloud the directions, and have children work independently or with a partner to write words with *oi* or *oy*.

Day 5 — Complete the Sort

Whole Group/Independent

Paste in Place

Have children turn to page 113 in their Word Study Notebook. Encourage children to sort their words by spelling patterns *oi* and *oy*. Then have them paste the words in the correct column on the page.

Play the Game

When children are finished, they may play Treasure Hunt. (See the Teacher Resource CD for the game board, word list, spinner, and directions.)

Building Vocabulary

Explain that *moist* means "wet." Ask children to think of things that could be *moist*. *(sweaty hands, sponges, bathing suits)*

ESL/ELL English Language Learners

Review the words with children. Explain that *Roy* begins with a capital letter because it is a person's name and Troy begins with a capital letter because it is a person's name and the name of a city. Have children say the different words to be sure they understand that the vowel sound in words with *oi* or *oy* are pronounced identically.

Challenge Words Activity

Ask children to name other words with *oi* or *oy*. If children need prompting, make suggestions from the Challenge Words list. Then have children use a blank grid to make word cards for these new words. Have children add them to the words for the sort and then re-sort all the words by spelling pattern.

Teacher Tip

Encourage children to develop their sorting skills by practicing with common objects (pencils, articles of clothing, colors, shapes, and so on) in the classroom.

Vowel Digraph oo

Objectives:

- To identify ŏŏ and o͞o = u vowel sounds
- To read, sort, and write words with sounds spelled ŏŏ or o͞o = u

Materials

 Big Book of Rhymes, Level B, "The Puppet Show," page 61

 Teacher Resource CD, Level B, Sort 29

 Word Study Notebook, Level B, pages 115–118

 Words Their Way Library, Level B, *The Kite That Flew Away*

 Teacher Resource CD, Level B, Follow the Dragon

Words

ŏŏ	o͞o = u	oddball
nook	fool	would
brook	spoon	could
hook	stool	should
hood	root	
crook	troop	
wood	noon	
foot	hoop	
stood	spool	
wool	tool	
soot	groom	

Challenge Words

shook	coop
	droop
	spool
	snoop
	brood

Day 1 Introduce the Sort

Whole Group

 Read a Rhyme: "The Puppet Show"

As you read "The Puppet Show," emphasize the words that contain the target spelling pattern and sounds. *(wood, book, took; soon, noon)* Ask children to locate these words in the poem, and help them write the words in two columns on the board. Ask children how the words are alike.

 Introduce Word Sort Vowel Digraph oo

Print out and cut apart the word cards for Sort 29 from the Teacher Resource CD. Introduce the words, and define in context words that may be unfamiliar to children, such as *nook, brook, troop, groom,* and *soot.* Help children sort the words into ŏŏ and o͞o = u categories. Point out that *could, would,* and *should* are oddballs.

Day 2 Practice the Sort

Whole Group/Independent/Partner

 You may want to begin Days 2–5 by reading the rhyme from Day 1. Then review the previous day's sort demonstration. Then help children tear out page 115 from their Word Study Notebook and cut apart the word cards.

Have children work independently or with a partner to say the words and, using the grid on page 117 of their Word Study Notebook, sort the words by ŏŏ and o͞o = u vowel sounds.

Alternative Sort: Brainstorming

Ask children to think of other words that that contain oo. Write their responses on the board. When children have completed brainstorming, ask them to identify and sort all the words they named by ŏŏ and o͞o = u vowel sounds.

Day 3 | Find Words in Context

Whole Group/Independent/Partner

Have children re-sort their cards. Read *The Kite That Flew Away* with children. Have children listen for and identify any words that contain ŏŏ or ōō = u spelling patterns. *(took, look)* Then have children identify words in the story that have the same vowel sound as *spoon* and *noon*. *(Sue, blue, glue, clue, blew, new, drew)* Point out that the oo = u vowel sound in these words is spelled *ew* and *ue*.

Day 4 | Apply the Skill

Independent/Partner

Have children sort their cards again. Ask children to brainstorm other ŏŏ (short vowel symbol) and ōō (long vowel symbol) = u words. Then have them turn to page 118 in their Word Study Notebook. Read aloud the directions, and have children work independently or with a partner to choose beginning and ending letters to form ŏŏ and ōō = u words.

Day 5 | Complete the Sort

Whole Group/Independent

Paste in Place

Have children turn to page 117 in their Word Study Notebook. Encourage children to sort their words according to ŏŏ and ōō = u vowel sounds. Then have them paste the words in the correct column on the page.

Play the Game

When children are finished, they may play Follow the Dragon. (See the Teacher Resource CD for the game board, Dragon Scales sheet, spinner, and directions.)

Building Vocabulary

Explain that *soot* is the black powder left after a fire. Point out that children would need to wash their hands if they got soot on them.

ESL/ELL English Language Learners

Review the words with children. You may need to explain that a *nook* is a type of hidden place, and that *groom* can have several meanings, including a person who takes care of horses and the man who marries a bride. Have children repeat after you each word in the sort to be sure they are differentiating between the ŏŏ and ōō = u words.

Challenge Words Activity

Ask children to name other words that contain oo. If children need prompting, make suggestions from the Challenge Words list. Then have children draw the outline of a book and a stool on paper. Have them write ŏŏ Challenge Words on the book and ōō = u Challenge Words on the stool.

Teacher Tip

Provide extra practice with identifying ŏŏ and ōō = u sounds by showing four word cards, three of which have the same vowel sound and one that has a different vowel sound. Challenge students to identify the word card that doesn't belong. Repeat with other word cards.

Objectives:

- To identify *aw* and *au* vowel sounds
- To read, sort, and write words with sounds spelled *aw* or *au*

Materials

 Big Book of Rhymes, Level B, "The Lobster Boats," page 63

 Teacher Resource CD, Level B, Sort 30

 Word Study Notebook, Level B, pages 119–122

 Words Their Way Library, Level B, *Lobster Fishing at Dawn*

 Teacher Resource CD, Level B, Spelling Match

Words		
aw	au	oddball
straw	haul	laugh
paw	taught	
yawn	sauce	
draw	vault	
crawl	fault	
raw	pause	
hawk	launch	
law	cause	
claw	haunt	
lawn	maul	

Challenge Words	
bawl	caught
fawn	haunch
sprawl	
thaw	

Day 1   Introduce the Sort

Whole Group

Read a Rhyme: "The Lobster Boats"

As you read "The Lobster Boats," emphasize the words that have the target sound (*dawn, haul, awesome, claws*). Have children locate these words in the poem. Write the words in a column on the board. Ask children why you should move one of the words into a second column. (The word *haul* is spelled with *au*.)

Introduce Word Sort Vowel Digraphs *aw, au*

Print out and cut apart the word cards for Sort 30 from the Teacher Resource CD. Introduce the words, and define in context words that may be unfamiliar to children, such as *haunt, claw, vault, maul,* and *launch.* Help children sort the words by *aw* and *au* spelling patterns. Point out that *laugh* is an oddball because it has the same spelling pattern as *haul* but a different pronunciation.

Day 2   Practice the Sort

Whole Group/Independent/Partner

You may want to begin Days 2–5 by reading the rhyme from Day 1. Then review the previous day's sort demonstration. Then help children tear out page 119 from their Word Study Notebook and cut apart the word cards.

Have children work independently or with a partner to say the words and, using the grid on page 121 of their Word Study Notebook, sort the words by spelling pattern.

Alternative Sort: Action Words

When children are comfortable with this week's sort, ask them to sort the words by those that show an action and those that do not. (*yawn, draw, crawl, haul, vault, launch, laugh*)

Day 3

Find Words in Context

Whole Group /Independent/Partner

Have children re-sort their cards. Read *Lobster Fishing at Dawn* with children. Have children listen for and identify any words that contain the same vowel sound as the word *dawn*. *(raw, haul, crawl, claws, caught)* Then have children look through their word cards to find ones that match words in the text. *(crawl, raw, haul, claw)*

Day 4

Apply the Skill

Independent/Partner

Have children sort their cards again. Ask children to brainstorm other words with *aw* or *au*. Then have them turn to page 122 in their Word Study Notebook. Read aloud the directions, and have children work independently or with a partner to choose beginning and ending letters to write words with *aw* or *au*.

Day 5

Complete the Sort

Whole Group/Independent

Paste in Place

Have children turn to page 121 in their Word Study Notebook. Encourage children to sort their words by spelling patterns *aw* and *au*. Then have them paste the words in the correct column on the grid.

Play the Game

When children are finished, they may play Spelling Match. (See the Teacher Resource CD for the game card/answer sheet and directions.)

Building Vocabulary

Explain that *launch* means "to send off or to send afloat." Point out that people might launch a rocket or they might launch a ship. Tell children that a *launch* can also be a small, open-decked motorboat. Invite children to act out launching a toy rocket.

ESL/ELL English Language Learners

Direct children's attention to the words *laugh* and *taught*. Explain that in some words, *gh* is silent *(taught, knight)* and in other words, *gh* has the *f* sound *(laugh, cough)*. Explain that each time children encounter a new word with *gh*, they must learn and memorize how the word is pronounced.

Challenge Words Activity

Together, make a list of other words that contain *aw* or *au*. If children need prompting, make suggestions from the Challenge Words list. Read aloud the list of words. Then invite children to take turns giving a clue for a word. Have others in the group identify the word.

Teacher Tip

Children may benefit by making picture cards for some of the words. Tell children to illustrate words such as *laugh*, *paw*, and *yawn* on index cards. Then have them trade their picture cards with a partner and match them with word cards.

Diphthongs ou, ow

Objectives:

- To identify *ou* and *ow* vowel sounds
- To read, sort, and write words with sounds spelled *ou* or *ow*

Materials

Big Book of Rhymes, Level B, "New Jeans Now!," page 65

Teacher Resource CD, Level B, Sort 31

Word Study Notebook, Level B, pages 123–126

Words Their Way Library, Level B, *Where Jeans Come From*

Teacher Resource CD, Level B, One Card!

Words

ou	ow	oddball
pound	clown	tough
mouth	town	rough
south	frown	grown
ground	howl	
couch	owl	
count	drown	
shout	growl	
cloud	plow	
scout	crown	
found	gown	

Challenge Words

drought	fowl	touch
foul	prowl	
stout	scowl	
	brow	

Day 1 Introduce the Sort

Whole Group

Read a Rhyme: "New Jeans Now!"

Read the poem "New Jeans Now!" Write *brown* on the board as a column header, and have children name other words in the poem that have the same vowel sound. *(how, now, out)* Write these words in the column. Ask children why you should move one of the words into a second column. (The word *out* has a different spelling for the sound.)

Introduce Word Sort Diphthongs *ou, ow*

Print out and cut apart the word cards for Sort 31 from the Teacher Resource CD. Introduce the words, defining in context any that may be unfamiliar to children, such as *tough, howl, scout,* and *couch*. Help children sort the words into three categories: words with *ou* as in *sound,* words with *ow* as in *brown,* and words with different sounds spelled with *ou* or *ow*.

Day 2 Practice the Sort

Whole Group/Independent/Partner

You may want to begin Days 2–5 by reading the rhyme from Day 1. Then review the previous day's sort demonstration. Then help children tear out page 123 from their Word Study Notebook and cut apart the word cards.

Have children work independently or with a partner to say the words and, using the grid on page 125 of their Word Study Notebook, sort the words by *ou* and *ow* patterns.

Alternative Sort: Noun, Verb, or Both?

Using the word cards, demonstrate each word's use in a sentence. Point out that some words can be a noun or a verb. *(pound, ground, frown, howl, count, growl, crown, plow, cloud, scout, mouth,* and *clown)* Let children take over the sort and categorize words as nouns, verbs, or both.

3 Find Words in Context

Whole Group/Independent/Partner

Have children re-sort their cards. Read *Where Jeans Come From* with children. Have children listen for and identify words with the same vowel sound as the word *sound. (around, out, ground, about, flowers, cloud, how, mounds, now)* Point out that *flowers, how,* and *now* have the same vowel sound as *sound,* but the sound is spelled with *ow* instead of *ou.* You might also point out that other words in the story have *ow* but have the long *o* vowel sound *(grow, know, shows).*

Day
4 Apply the Skill

Independent/Partner

Have children sort their cards again. Ask children to brainstorm other words with *ou* or *ow.* Then have them turn to page 126 in their Word Study Notebook. Read aloud the directions, and have children work independently or with a partner to choose beginning and ending letters to write words with *ou* or *ow.*

Day
5 Complete the Sort

Whole Group/Independent/Partner

Paste in Place

Have children turn to page 125 in their Word Study Notebook. Encourage children to sort the words by *ou* and *ow* patterns. Then have children paste the words in the correct column on the page.

Play the Game

When children are finished, they may play One Card! (See the Teacher Resource CD for the playing cards and directions.)

Building Vocabulary

Ask children which of the sort words means a piece of furniture. Invite children to describe a couch so everyone understands what it is, and then have them tell another word they know for the same object. *(sofa)*

ESL/ELL English Language Learners

Practice with children the pronunciation of any target words that they may find troublesome by studying them within sets of rhyming word cards, such as *pound, ground,* and *found.* Study a set at a time, calling attention to the spelling pattern. Have children make sentences for each word and draw a sketch for each.

Challenge Words Activity

Encourage pairs of children to hunt for additional *ou* and *ow* words in magazines and newspapers. Have children write their words on blank cards to share with the group. Combine the new cards with the week's word cards, and re-sort them by *ou* and *ow* patterns. Have volunteers count the number of words in each sort.

Teacher Tip

Encourage partners to take turns flashing the cards for a specified number of seconds. Have each reader count the cards that were read correctly and record the final number. See if children can read the cards faster another day.

Spell Check 5

After completing sorts 28–31, you may want to administer Spell Check 5 in the Word Study Notebook on page 151. See pages 21–22 for instructions on progress monitoring and using Spell Checks.

Silent Beginning Consonants kn, wr, gn

Objectives:

- To identify sounds of *kn, wr,* or *gn*
- To read, sort, and write words with *kn, wr,* and *gn*

Materials

Big Book of Rhymes, Level B, "My Puppy Gus," page 67

Teacher Resource CD, Level B, Sort 32

Word Study Notebook, Level B, pages 127–130

Words Their Way Library, Level B, *Flip's Trick*

Teacher Resource CD, Level B, Use Those Clues

Words

kn	wr	gn	oddball
known	wreck	gnaw	rap
knit	wreath	gnash	ring
knot	wren		
knight	wrist		
knob	wrinkle		
knee	wring		
knead	wrap		

Challenge Words

knew	wrong	gnarl
knelt	wreak	gnu
knock	writer	gnome
knife		

Day 1 Introduce the Sort

Whole Group

Read a Rhyme: "My Puppy Gus"

As you read the poem "My Puppy Gus," point out the word *wriggle,* and ask children what they notice about this word's beginning sound and spelling. Repeat with words *gnats, gnaws,* and *know.* Write these words on the board, and underline their beginning consonants. Help children understand that each of the first consonants in these letter patterns is silent.

Introduce Word Sort Silent Beginning Consonants *kn, wr, gn*

Print out and cut apart the word cards for Sort 32 from the Teacher Resource CD. Introduce the words, and define in context words that may be unfamiliar to children, such as w*ren, gnaw, knead,* and *gnash.* Read each word and help children sort the words by silent beginning consonants. Point out that *rap* and *ring* are oddballs because their beginning consonants aren't silent.

Day 2 Practice the Sort

Whole Group/Independent/Partner

You may want to begin Days 2–5 by reading the rhyme from Day 1. Then review the previous day's sort demonstration. Then help children tear out page 127 from their Word Study Notebook and cut apart the word cards.

Have children work independently or with a partner to say the words and, using the grid on page 129 of their Word Study Notebook, sort the words by beginning sound and its spelling.

Alternative Sort: Homophone Challenge

Call attention to words *wrap* and *rap.* Remind children that these words are homophones beause they sound alike but have different meanings and spellings. Have children find the other homophones in the sort. *(wring* and *ring)* Then challenge children to make homophone word cards for other words in the sort. *(night, need)*

Find Words in Context

Whole Group/Partner

Have children re-sort their cards. Read *Flip's Trick* with children. Have children listen and identify any words with silent beginning consonants. *(know)* Have children work with a partner to find and read their word cards that have the same beginning sound and spelling as *know*. *(knit, knot, knight, knob, knee, knead, knife)*

Apply the Skill

Independent/Partner

Have children sort their cards again. Then have them turn to page 130 in their Word Study Notebook. Read aloud the directions, and have children work independently or with a partner to write and illustrate words with *kn, wr,* or *gn*.

Complete the Sort

Whole Group/Independent

Paste in Place

Have children turn to page 129 in their Word Study Notebook. Encourage children to sort their cards by beginning sound and its spelling. Then have them paste the words in the correct column on the page.

Play the Game

When children are finished, they may play Use Those Clues. (See the Teacher Resource CD for the game board, playing cards, and directions.)

Building Vocabulary

Ask children if they have heard someone say an animal can *gnaw* something. Clarify the meaning of *gnaw* by having children suggest and pantomime gnawing animals, such as dogs, mice, beavers, lions, or any animals in your area. Children can be challenged to use this meaning of *gnaw* for telling how a feeling such as hunger or worry can gnaw at people.

ESL/ELL English Language Learners

Review with children the homophones they have learned this week: *wrap* and *rap, wring* and *ring, knot* and *not, knight* and *night, knead* and *need*. Help children make sentences such as "The knight rides in the night," to familiarize them with meaning, usage, and spelling of these homophones.

Challenge Words Activity

Ask children to name other words that begin with *kn, wr,* or *gn*. If children need prompting, suggest words from the Challenge Words list. Have children make word cards for the new words. Substitute these cards for some of the Sort 32 cards, and have children sort them into categories that they establish.

Teacher Tip

During repeated sorts, do not immediately correct children's mispronunciations of the target sounds. Instead, have them reread the column to correct their own mistakes. If further help is still needed, draw their attention to the same initial spelling in a word they have pronounced correctly.

Triple r-Blends scr, str, spr

Objectives:

- To identify blended sounds of *scr*, *str*, and *spr*
- To read, sort, and write words with *scr*, *str*, or *spr*

Materials

 Big Book of Rhymes, Level B, "The Journey," page 69

 Teacher Resource CD, Level B, Sort 33

 Word Study Notebook, Level B, pages 131–134

 Words Their Way Library, Level B, *Heather's Book*

 Teacher Resource CD, Level B, Island Hop

Words

scr	str	spr	oddball
scrap	stress	spray	squirrel
scream	strict	spruce	
scrape	straight	sprout	
scram	string	spread	
scribe	strange		
script	stripe		
scratch	stretch		

Challenge Words

scramble	stride	sprawl
scroll	strewn	sprung
	stroll	spry
	stream	

Day 1 Introduce the Sort

Whole Group

 Read a Rhyme: "The Journey"

To introduce words that begin with *scr*, *str*, or *spr*, read the poem "The Journey." Read the poem again, emphasizing the words *stroke*, *strange*, *spray*, and *scraps*. Call children's attention to how the first three letters in each of these words are pronounced as blended sounds. Write the words on the board, underline the triple *r*-blends, and have children name the three-letter pattern at the beginning of these words. Encourage children to tell other words they know that begin with these blends.

 Introduce Word Sort Triple *r*-Blends scr, str, spr

Print out and cut apart the word cards for Sort 33 from the Teacher Resource CD. Introduce the words, and define in context words that may be unfamiliar to children, such as *spruce, sprout, scribe,* and *script*. Help children sort the words by beginning blend, noting that *squirrel* is an oddball word. Reread the columns with children, and have them explain the sort.

Day 2 Practice the Sort

Whole Group/Independent/Partner

 You may want to begin Days 2–5 by reading the rhyme from Day 1. Then review the previous day's sort demonstration. Then help children tear out page 131 from their Word Study Notebook and cut apart the word cards.

Have children work independently or with a partner to say the words and, using the grid on page 133 of their Word Study Notebook, sort the words by beginning sounds spelled *scr, str,* and *spr*.

Alternative Sort: Vowel Sounds

When children are comfortable with this week's sort, have children sort the words by vowel sound. Suggest they make short, long, and *r*-influenced vowel columns, they can establish vowel categories, or they can guess the categorizing that you establish. Then have children complete the sort.

Find Words in Context

Whole Group/Independent

Have children re-sort their cards. Read *Heather's Book* with children. Have them listen for and identify words that begin like *stripe* and *spray*. *(stream, spread, spring)* Have children find their word card for *spread* and then read their other words that begin with the *spr* blend sound. Then have children find and read the word cards that begin like *stream*.

Day

4

Apply the Skill

Independent/Partner

Have children sort their cards again. Then have them turn to page 134 in their Word Study Notebook. Read aloud the directions and have children work independently or with a partner to write words beginning with *scr, str,* or *spr* blends. Explain that they may use words from the sort or words they think of on their own.

Day

5

Complete the Sort

Whole Group/Independent

Paste in Place

Have children turn to page 133 in their Word Study Notebook. Encourage children to sort their cards by beginning blends *scr, str,* and *spr*. Then have them paste the words in the correct column on the page.

Play the Game

When children are finished, they may play Island Hop. (See the Teacher Resource CD for the game board, playing cards, spinner, and directions.)

Building Vocabulary

Ask children what a spruce is. You may need to clarify that it is an evergreen tree before saying that this word has another meaning too. Have children figure out what the word means when you ask "Do you spruce up your room when it is messy?" Have children work in pairs, taking turns making sentences with the word and deciding which meaning the speaker is using.

ESL/ELL English Language Learners

Inclusion and pronunciation of the *r* sound in these blends may be problematic. If so, help children become more aware of how the blends are produced differently in the mouth and practice sets of words such as *ring-spring-string, rap-scrap-strap,* and *rain-strain-sprain.*

Challenge Words Activity

Help children brainstorm other words that begin with *scr, str,* or *spr.* If children need prompting, suggest words from the Challenge Words list. Then have children make word cards for these new words, sort them by beginning blend, and reread the columns aloud. An additional challenge can be to re-sort the words into different categories.

Teacher Tip

For practice or informal assessment, give children *scr, str,* and *spr* cards. Have children hold up the blend they hear as you say a word.

Consonant Digraphs Plus r-Blends and squ

Objectives:

- To identify *thr*, *shr*, and *squ* blends
- To read, sort, and write words with *thr*, *shr*, or *squ*

Materials

 Big Book of Rhymes, Level B, "Running Squirrels," page 71

 Teacher Resource CD, Level B, Sort 34

 Word Study Notebook, Level B, pages 135–138

 Words Their Way Library, Level B, Squirrels

 Teacher Resource CD, Level B, Clues and Categories

Words

thr	shr	squ
throne	shrink	squirm
threw	shrub	squint
threat	shrug	squeak
throw	shriek	squeeze
thrill	shrunk	squish
through	shrewd	squash
thrifty	shrimp	squawk

Challenge Words

thread	shred	squall
thrash	shrill	square
thrive	shrivel	squirt

Introduce the Sort

Whole Group

 Read a Rhyme: "Running Squirrels"

Read the poem "Running Squirrels" to introduce words with consonant blends *thr*, *shr*, and *squ*. Emphasize the words *shrubs* and *through*. Call attention to *sh* and *th* followed by *r* and how these sounds are pronounced as blended sounds. Remind children that *u* always follows *q*, even though it is not heard in the beginning blend of *squirrels*. Encourage children to tell other words they know that begin with these blended sounds.

 Introduce Word Sort Consonant Digraphs Plus r-Blends and squ

Print out and cut apart the word cards for Sort 34 from the Teacher Resource CD. Introduce the words, and define in context words that may be unfamiliar to children, such as *shrug*, *shriek*, *squint*, *shrewd*, and *thrifty*. Help children sort the words by beginning blend. Reread the columns with children, and have them explain the sort.

Practice the Sort

Whole Group/Independent/Partner

 You may want to begin Days 2–5 by reading the rhyme from Day 1. Then review the previous day's sort demonstration. Then help children tear out page 135 from their Word Study Notebook and cut apart the word cards.

Have children work independently or with a partner to say the words and, using the grid on page 137 of their Word Study Notebook, sort the words by beginning sounds.

Alternative Sort: Nouns and Actions

The word card for *through* should not be used for this sort. The remaining word cards can be sorted into categories of things, actions happening now, and actions that have already happened. If children notice that words such as *shrug*, *squint*, and *shriek* can be a thing or an action, encourage them to make extra cards and place the words in both categories.

Day 3

Find Words in Context

Whole Group/Independent/Partner

Have children re-sort their cards. Read *Squirrels* with children. During a second reading, have them emphasize *squirrels* and *squirrel* each time the words are read. Have children use their word cards independently or with a partner to create sentences about squirrels, such as "I saw a squirrel squeeze into a tiny hole."

Day 4

Apply the Skill

Independent/Partner

Have children sort their cards again. Then have them turn to page 138 in their Word Study Notebook. Read aloud the directions, and have children work independently or with a partner to write words beginning with *thr, shr,* or *squ.* Explain that they may use words from the sort or words they think of on their own.

Day 5

Complete the Sort

Whole Group/Independent/Partner

Paste in Place

Have children turn to page 137 in their Word Study Notebook. Encourage children to sort the words by the beginning blends *thr, shr,* and *squ.* Then have them paste the words in the correct column on the grid.

Play the Game

When children are finished, they may play Clues and Categories. (See the Teacher Resource CD for the game board, playing cards, and directions.)

Building Vocabulary

Write *thrifty* on the board, cover the *y,* and ask children if they know what *thrift* means. Define it if necessary, and then uncover the *y.* Have children tell how the meaning is changed, as in "I try to be thrifty with the money I earn." Encourage children to complete "We can be thrifty by _____" in different ways.

ESL/ELL English Language Learners

Clarify differences in meaning between *squirm/shrug/squint* and *shriek/squeak/squawk* through pantomime and discussion. You might also point out that, although *squash* and *squish* can mean "to press," we usually use *squish* when talking about pressing something wet and the sound that is made as a result.

Challenge Words Activity

Help children brainstorm other words that begin with *thr, shr,* or *squ.* If children need prompting, make suggestions from the Challenge Words list. Then have children make word cards for these new words. They can work with a partner to sort the words into categories.

Teacher Tip

Be sure that children understand the difference between *threw* and *through.* Have children hold up the appropriate word card as you say sentences for each homophone.

Sort 35

Hard and Soft c and g

Objectives:

- To identify two sounds of c and g
- To read, sort, and write words with hard or soft c or g

Materials

Big Book of Rhymes, Level B, "Goose Goes to the City," page 73

Teacher Resource CD, Level B, Sort 35

Word Study Notebook, Level B, pages 139–142

Words Their Way Library, Level B, *The City Cat and the Country Cat*

Teacher Resource CD, Level B, Category Challenge

Words

hard c	soft c	hard g	soft g
coat	center	guess	gym
cub	circle	guide	gentle
carrot	cent	game	gem
cart	cell	guest	giraffe
code	circus	golf	gist
calf	cycle	goose	ginger

Challenge Words

candle	ceiling	gulf	giant
cactus	cease	guard	gesture
castle	certain	garden	germ
comb	cyclone	gulp	gently

Day 1 Introduce the Sort

Whole Group

Read a Rhyme: "Goose Goes to the City"

Read the poem "Goose Goes to the City" to introduce words with the hard or soft sounds of c or g. Then begin a four-column list on the board by writing *country* and *goose* as headings of columns 1 and 3. Have children name other words that begin with the same hard sounds of c and g (cars), and add them to the appropriate column on the board. Then have children identify c and g words that have soft sounds and make these headings of columns 2 and 4. (city, giraffe)

Introduce Word Sort Hard and Soft c and g

Print out and cut apart the word cards for Sort 35 from the Teacher Resource CD. Introduce the words, and define in context words that may be unfamiliar to children, such as *gem, gist,* and *ginger*. Help children sort the words by beginning hard and soft c and g sounds.

Day 2 Practice the Sort

Whole Group/Independent/Partner

You may want to begin Days 2–5 by reading the rhyme from Day 1. If you wish, review with children the previous day's word sort demonstration. Then help children tear out page 139 from their Word Study Notebook and cut apart the word cards.

Have children work independently or with a partner to say the words and, using the grid on page 141 of their Word Study Notebook, sort the words by beginning sounds.

Alternative Sort: Sorting By Vowels

After children are comfortable with this week's sort, ask them to sort the cards by first vowel. Ask children to put all the cards with a first vowel of *a, o,* or *u* in one pile and words with *e, i,* or *y* in another pile. Discuss the new sorts. Help children realize that the vowel that follows c or g determines the hard or soft sound.

3 Find Words in Context

Whole Group/Independent/Partner

Have children re-sort their cards. Read *The City Cat and the Country Cat* with children. Have them listen for and identify words that begin with hard and soft *c*, as in *cat* and *city*. Have children work independently or with a partner to reread the book and make a list of all the hard c words *(cat, country, can, camp, come, cab)* and all the soft c words *(city, circle, circus)* in the story.

Day

4 Apply the Skill

Independent/Partner

Have children sort their cards again. Then have them turn to page 142 in their Word Study Notebook. Read aloud the directions, and have children work independently or with a partner to say each word and write it in the box with corresponding consonant sound.

Day

5 Complete the Sort

Whole Group/Independent/Partner

Paste in Place

Have children turn to page 141 in their Word Study Notebook. Encourage children to sort the words by hard and soft c and g. Then have them paste the words in the correct column on the grid.

Play the Game

When children are finished, they may play Category Challenge. (See the Teacher Resource CD for the playing cards and directions.)

Building Vocabulary

Use stories and articles that children have recently read to make statements using the word *gist*. Ask children what *gist* means. When they figure out that it means "the main idea," have them make statements about the gist of other texts. Then ask what the gist of a discussion or a speech might be.

ESL/ELL English Language Learners

Hold up word cards as you help children practice the usage of words that are problematic for them. Model using a word in a sentence, and then have children repeat the sentence after you. Then ask questions such as "Do you like to eat a *carrot* with your lunch?" and have each child respond, using the word in his or her answer.

Challenge Words Activity

Have children name other words that begin with hard or soft *c* or *g*. If children need prompting, make suggestions from the Challenge Words list. Then have children make word cards for these new words. They can work with a partner to sort the words into categories.

Teacher Tip

Word cards of nouns can be used in a "tell something you know about it" circle game for small groups. Each child in turn tells a different fact or must hold the card as play continues with other words. After the game, children holding cards use nonfiction texts to find a new fact to report back to the group.

Sort 36

Word Endings -ce, -ve, -se

Objectives:

- To identify final sounds /s/, /v/, and /z/
- To read, sort, and write words ending in -ce, -ve, or -se

Materials

 Big Book of Rhymes, Level B, "Once Upon a Time," page 75

 Teacher Resource CD, Level B, Sort 36

 Word Study Notebook, Level B, pages 143–146

 Words Their Way Library, Level B, *Once Upon a Time*

 Teacher Resource CD, Level B, Castle Maze

Words

-ce	-ve	-se
glance	twelve	sense
prince	leave	choose
piece	prove	wise
bounce	glove	cheese
peace	solve	tease
dance	love	loose
since	shove	those

Challenge Words

since	serve	surprise
surface	above	dense
twice	drive	nurse
voice	brave	purchase

Day 1 Introduce the Sort

Whole Group

Read a Rhyme: "Once Upon a Time"

To introduce words ending in -ce, -ve, or -se, read the poem "Once Upon a Time." Point out the word *Once*, and ask children what they notice about its final sound and its spelling. Do the same for *cave* and *chose*. Help children understand that these words are spelled with a silent e. Then have children find other words in the poem that end like *Once* and *cave*. (*nice, prince, brave*)

Introduce Word Sort -ce, -ve, -se

Print out and cut apart the word cards for Sort 36 from the Teacher Resource CD. Introduce the words, and define in context words that may be unfamiliar to children, such as *glance, solve,* and *shove*. Then demonstrate sorting the words by final -ce, -ve, and -se. Reread the columns with children, and challenge them to figure out something about the words that end in -se. (The -se can either have the /s/ sound or the /z/ sound.)

Day 2 Practice the Sort

Whole Group/Independent/Partner

You may want to begin Days 2–5 by reading the rhyme from Day 1. If you wish, review with children the previous day's word sort demonstration. Then help children tear out page 143 from their Word Study Notebook and cut apart the word cards.

Have children work independently or with a partner to say the words and, using the grid on page 145 of their Word Study Notebook, sort the words by end sound and spelling.

Alternative Sort: Guess My Category

Begin sorting words into the following categories: a beginning single consonant, a beginning digraph, and a beginning blend. When children recognize the categories, let them complete the sort.

94

Day 3 — Find Words in Context

Whole Group/Independent/Partner

Have children re-sort their cards. Read *Once Upon a Time* with children. Have children listen for and identify words that end with *-ce* and *-se*, (*once, house*)

Have children work independently or with a partner to find and read all of their word cards that end with /s/ spelled *-ce* or *-se* as in *once* and *house*. (*sense, glance, prince, piece, bounce, peace, loose, dance, fence*)

Day 4 — Apply the Skill

Independent/Partner

Have children sort their cards again. Then have them turn to page 146 in their Word Study Notebook. Read aloud the directions, and have children work independently or with a partner to choose beginning and middle letters to write words that end with *-ce*, *-ve*, or *-se*.

Day 5 — Complete the Sort

Whole Group/Independent/Partner

Paste in Place

Have children turn to page 145 in their Word Study Notebook. Encourage children to sort their words by word endings *-ce*, *-ve*, or *-se*. Then have them paste the words in the correct column on the page.

Play the Game

When children are finished, they may play Castle Maze. (See the Teacher Resource CD for the playing cards and directions.)

Building Vocabulary

Ask children what a *glance* is. You may need to clarify that it is a quick look before explaining that this word has other meanings, too. Have children figure out the differences in meaning when you ask "Do you glance at things as you ride in a car?" and "Have you ever seen a basketball glance off a backboard?" Have children take turns making sentences with the word and deciding which meaning the speaker is using.

ESL/ELL English Language Learners

Check that children are saying the final sound of each word correctly, especially the /s/ or /z/ spelled *-se*. Help them practice one set of words that share the same final sound and spelling at a time.

Challenge Words Activity

Have children name other words that end in *-ce*, *-ve*, or *-se*. If children need prompting, make suggestions from the Challenge Words list. Then have children make word cards for these new words. They can work with a partner to sort the words into categories.

Teacher Tip

Be sure that children understand the difference between *piece* and *peace*. Have them hold up the appropriate word card as you say sentences with each homophone.

Spell Check 6

After completing sorts 32–36, you may want to administer Spell Checks 6A (Beginning Complex Consonant Clusters) and 6B (Hard and Soft *c* and *g* Word Endings *-ce*, *-se*, and *-ve*) in the Word Study Notebook on pages 152–153. See pages 21–22 for instructions on progress monitoring and using the Spell Check.